CLASSICS IN EDUCATION
Lawrence A. Cremin, General Editor

☆ ☆ ☆

P9-DHC-941

PSYCHOLOGY AND THE SCIENCE OF EDUCATION
Selected Writings of Edward L. Thorndike
Edited by Geraldine M. Joncich

THE NEW-ENGLAND PRIMER
Introduction by Paul Leicester Ford

BENJAMIN FRANKLIN ON EDUCATION
Edited by John Hardin Best

THE COLLEGES AND THE PUBLIC
1787–1862
Edited by Theodore Rawson Crane

TRADITIONS OF AFRICAN EDUCATION
Edited by David G. Scanlon

NOAH WEBSTER'S AMERICAN SPELLING BOOK
Introductory Essay by Henry Steele Commager

VITTORINO DA FELTRE
AND OTHER HUMANIST EDUCATORS
By William Harrison Woodward
Foreword by Eugene F. Rice, Jr.

DESIDERIUS ERASMUS
CONCERNING THE AIM AND METHOD
OF EDUCATION
By William Harrison Woodward
Foreword by Craig R. Thompson

JOHN LOCKE ON EDUCATION
Edited by Peter Gay

CATHOLIC EDUCATION IN AMERICA
A Documentary History
Edited by Neil G. McCluskey, S.J.

THE AGE OF THE ACADEMIES
Edited by Theodore R. Sizer

HEALTH, GROWTH, AND HEREDITY
G. Stanley Hall on Natural Education
Edited by Charles E. Strickland and Charles Burgess

TEACHER EDUCATION IN AMERICA
A Documentary History
Edited by Merle L. Borrowman

Sir James Kay-Shuttleworth
on Popular Education

Edited, with an Introduction and Notes, by
TRYGVE R. THOLFSEN

CLASSICS IN

No. 49

EDUCATION

TEACHERS COLLEGE PRESS
TEACHERS COLLEGE, COLUMBIA UNIVERSITY
NEW YORK AND LONDON

© 1974 by Teachers College
Columbia University

Library of Congress Catalogue
Card Number 73-15046

Manufactured in the United States of America

Foreword

"Under his able administration the measures of the Committee of Council have been framed, and under his instructions and correspondence, these measures have become almost a national system of education." Thus did Henry Barnard characterize the achievement of his contemporary Sir James Kay-Shuttleworth—in effect, likening him to his own revered mentor Horace Mann. Yet the work of Kay-Shuttleworth has not been well remembered by American educators. The Mills, Matthew Arnold, and Henry Brougham in England, Friedrich Froebel, Victor Cousin, and François Guizot on the Continent, Domingo Sarmiento in Latin America—these are the nineteenth-century figures who parade through American histories of Western education as the foreign counterparts of the so-called common-school reformers.

The reasons are intriguing to contemplate. In part, English historians of education have themselves traditionally underrated Kay-Shuttleworth's accomplishments. A. E. Dobbs mentioned him only in the footnotes of *Education and Social Movements, 1700–1850,* while Charles Birchenough gave him what was at best a brief and scattered treatment in his *History of Elementary Education in England and Wales from 1800 to the Present Day.* It is only in the more recent reappraisals of John Hurt, Brian Simon, Hugh M. Pollard, and others that Kay-Shuttleworth has begun to emerge as the major figure he surely was. In part, American historians seem to have preferred the heady idealism of a Brougham or a Froebel to the more mundane realism of a Kay-Shuttleworth. Most important, perhaps, they may have been troubled by Kay-Shuttleworth's paternalism. As Professor Tholfsen makes clear, there were significant similarities between the thought of Kay-Shuttleworth and his contemporary Horace Mann, though the vision Mann proffered of the nature and function of education was considerably more humane and equalitarian. It is a difference worth contemplating at a time when Mann himself has been under attack by revisionist historians as a partisan of social control too little interested in the noble goals he so eloquently articulated.

LAWRENCE A. CREMIN

Contents

Introduction

"If history judged men less by the noise than by the difference they make, it is hard to think of any name in the Victorian age which deserves to stand above or even beside Kay-Shuttleworth's." [1] G. M. Young's arresting judgment is a useful reminder of the importance of the work of James Kay-Shuttleworth as secretary of the Committee of the Privy Council on Education from 1839 to 1849. When he took office the education of the working classes in England was drifting aimlessly in the hands of two competing religious societies, Anglican and Nonconformist, which agreed only on the need to keep governmental intervention to a minimum. By the time of his retirement, the situation had been transformed. Despite influential opposition, Kay-Shuttleworth established an administrative structure which enabled the central government to support and shape the development of popular education. In exchange for an expanding flow of state funds, schools operated by the religious societies became part of an elaborate system—including pupil-teachers, training colleges, national certification, scholarships, and stipends—intended to set

[1] G. M. Young, *Victorian England: Portrait of an Age* (London, 1952), p. 89. See also H. C. Barnard, *A History of English Education from 1760* (London, 1961), p. 111; and M. E. Sadler's Introduction to F. Smith, *The Life and Work of Sir James Kay-Shuttleworth* (London, 1923), for comparable estimates of his work.

and maintain high standards. Only schools which submitted to government inspection were eligible to receive
grants. As a result of Kay-Shuttleworth's efforts, popular
education had been recognized as a national responsibility and the necessary administrative apparatus had
been constructed. With good reason, then, he has been
called "the architect of elementary education" in England and has taken his place in the pantheon of educational reformers.

But Kay-Shuttleworth approached popular education
from a point of view totally at odds with mid-twentieth-
century social values, and recent scholarship has emphasized aspects of his work that were glossed over in an
earlier preoccupation with the magnitude of his achievement.[2] Imbued with a narrowly middle-class conception
of the purpose of popular education, Kay-Shuttleworth
conceived of it as a means of combatting working-class
indolence, immorality, and radicalism. His immediate
goal was the preservation of public order and stability:
that is, maintaining the privileges and power of the
propertied classes against the threat from below. Education was to be an instrument of social control. His
belief in the importance of popular education was based
on the conviction that the poor themselves, by virtue
of improvidence rooted in ignorance and vice, were responsible for their own poverty. Similarly, he interpreted
every attempt by workingmen to assert their independ-

---

[2] See B. Simon, *Studies in the History of Education, 1780–1870*
(London, 1960), pp. 166–176, 337–338; R. Johnson, "Educational
Policy and Social Control in Early Victorian England," *Past and
Present*, No. 49 (1970); J. Hurt, *Education in Evolution: Church,
State, Society and Popular Education, 1800–1870* (London, 1971),
pp. 22–24, 112–113, 220. For a caustic comment on Kay-Shuttle-
worth's view of the poor see E. P. Thompson, *The Making of the
English Working Class* (New York, 1966), pp. 267–268.

ence and defend their rights as the unfortunate consequence of lack of knowledge of their true interests. From
these social and ideological premises it followed logically
that if the fabric of society was to be preserved, the
common people must be educated.

At first glance it might seem that we are dealing with
two conflicting interpretations which need to be reconciled. We might even be tempted to apply a rough dis-
count to each side, on the assumption that the truth
usually lies in some neutral ground between extremes.
In fact, however, both interpretations are essential to an
understanding of a man who embodied a striking juxta-
position of disparate values and attitudes. Thus, it is
necessary to preserve undiluted the realistic and sometimes astringent view of Kay-Shuttleworth which emerged
in reaction against the conventional portrait of him as
an educational reformer *pur sang*. There can be no
blinking the fact that his approach to popular education was based on a conception of the poor which expressed the prejudices of the propertied classes in particularly harsh and doctrinaire form. On the other
hand, however, having recognized the social basis of
Kay-Shuttleworth's educational policies, we cannot simply write him off as an exponent of middle-class domination who seized on education as a handy weapon in
the class struggle. On a number of points he transcended
the limitations inherent in his middle-class outlook.

It is precisely the tension between genuine idealism
and class interest that makes Kay-Shuttleworth so interesting. Despite his unquestioning acceptance of doctrines
which dictated a repressive policy toward the poor, he
managed to preserve intact his decent and humane instincts. He denounced the use of corporal punishment
in pauper schools at a time when it was a common prac-

tice in all schools. He took pride in the happiness that he saw in the faces of children in a pauper school under his supervision and attributed it to their confidence in the "kindness of all by whom they are surrounded." Similarly, although he set out to use education as a means of social control, he also saw it as an instrument of moral and intellectual improvement. It was in pursuit of these more exalted goals that he tried to develop an educational system of the highest standard. He sought out the best and most advanced teaching methods. In particular, he urged that rote learning be banished and that the children of the poor be given an education based on Pestalozzian principles. Despite a moralistic revulsion at the "depravity" of the poor, he remained confident of their latent rationality and virtue. His zeal for excellence in education sprang from this optimistic and progressive creed, rather than from the narrowly social objectives that he also had in mind. Hence, although he never abandoned his deeply middle-class attitudes, he constructed a system of popular education which the middle classes themselves came to consider much too ambitious for the needs of the working classes.

I

James Kay [3] was born in 1804, the son of a cotton manufacturer in Rochdale, in the heart of industrial Lancashire. His social roots were firmly planted in the upper bourgeoisie. An uncle was a banker; two cousins were Members of Parliament; one brother was a calico

[3] Kay added the name Shuttleworth when he married Janet Shuttleworth in 1842. For this and other biographical details, see Smith, *Life and Work*.

printer, two others were barristers. The family moved
to Salford, near Manchester, and Kay attended a local
Grammar School. At the age of fifteen, he was sent to
work in his uncle's bank in Rochdale, where he remained for three years. He taught in the Sunday school,
and eventually became superintendent of the boys' department. Having absorbed a deep religiosity from his
parents, both Independents, he entered actively into the
life of the Sunday school. Although one of the deacons
tried to persuade him to become a missionary, Kay had
"an eager thirst for knowledge, and longed to go to the
university to study science, history, and metaphysics."
In 1824 he entered the University of Edinburgh as a
medical student. He did excellent work and was elected
president of the Royal Medical Society, a student organ-
ization. Charles Darwin, who enrolled at Edinburgh in
the following year, was most impressed by him. He did
research in diseases of the chest and the cause of death
in cases of asphyxiation. In 1826 he was appointed an
assistant in the Edinburgh New Town Dispensary, where
he became familiar "with the foulest slums in which
this wretched population seemed to be continually
perishing." While in Edinburgh, Kay began to read
the political economists, who provided him with the
conceptual and ideological apparatus which was to de-
fine his view of the poor.

After receiving his medical degree in 1827, Kay moved
to Manchester, the capital city of the Industrial Revolution. There he continued to take an active interest in the
working classes, and became Senior Physician at a charity hospital in one of the poorest sections of the city.
While ministering to the medical needs of the poor,
he also maintained the sociological concerns that had
captured his attention in Edinburgh. He helped to found

the *North of England Medical Journal* and contributed a number of articles on both medical and social topics. The first of these articles was a refutation of a critique of Malthusian political economy. Others dealt with the physical condition of the poor and the effects on the lungs of cotton workers of foreign particles breathed in while working in the factories. Kay also found time for politics and in 1831 published an anonymous pamphlet in support of the Whig Reform Bill. In 1832 an outbreak of cholera brought him into the closest possible contact with poverty and disease. Out of this experience, interpreted in the light of his study of political economy, came his pioneering work, *The Moral and Physical Condition of the Working Classes Employed in the Cotton Manufacture in Manchester*. The publication of the pamphlet marked a shift in Kay's interests from medicine to broader social problems and ways of dealing with them. In 1833 he helped to found the Manchester Provident Society, which set out to instruct the poor in domestic economy and to encourage them to follow a program of systematic saving. The same year he was also active in the establishment of the Manchester Statistical Society, which was to conduct detailed investigations into social and economic conditions in the region. In 1835 he moved into the national scene when he accepted appointment as an Assistant Poor Law Commissioner.

Kay's pamphlet *The Moral and Physical Condition of the Working Classes Employed in the Cotton Manufacture in Manchester* is central to an understanding of the close connection between his social philosophy and his educational policies. The main conclusion that emerges from this detailed account of the ills afflicting the poor is that only education can provide a remedy. In the course of the pamphlet Kay arrives at this conclusion by a rather circuitous route, which illuminates important features of his thought. Even the order in which his argument unfolds is instructive. He begins with a compassionate description of the wretchedness of the Manchester working classes, along with a cogent analysis of the economic and social factors which have reduced them to that condition. But the workingmen appear only momentarily as the victims of material circumstances beyond their control. Almost immediately Kay traces their poverty—and even their susceptibility to disease—to their own moral and intellectual deficiencies, and makes plain the depth of his revulsion at their depravity. As we read the pamphlet we see his initial understanding and compassion become overlaid with moral and ideological categories which inhibit his humane instincts and impose a callous and moralistic view of the poor. It is in this bleak context, shaped by the imperatives of class and ideology, that Kay turned to popular education. In reading the pamphlet, however, we must also keep in mind that in the course of his career, although Kay never abandoned these social and ideological presuppositions, they did not prevent him from developing the more positive values to which he was also committed.

Kay begins his report with a compelling account of the miserable condition of the Manchester working classes. The factors predisposing the working population to susceptibility to disease are set forth plainly: bad diet, inadequate disposal of sewage, housing which leaves the inhabitants exposed to cold and moisture, and the physical exhaustion resulting from extremely long hours in factory or workshop. He emphasizes the high incidence of typhus on the worst streets, with their

"heaps of refuse or stagnant pools." Despite his faith
in the absolute value of commercial and industrial expansion, Kay spells out the disastrous human consequences of the factory system. Long hours of monotonous toil tend to reduce the worker to an animal existence; he often succumbs to "fatal demoralization" and
seeks solace in the gin shops. Kay also describes the
moral consequences of bad housing and unsanitary conditions, and argues that the physical causes of disease
operate indirectly, through their "reflex influence on the
manners." Finally, having identified the fundamental
causes of working-class susceptibility to disease, Kay demands police regulations to correct the flagrant neglect
of the streets and dwellings of the poor.

Kay is unable to maintain his initial position throughout the report. As soon as the moral aspects of the problem engage his attention, his perspective shifts to that
of moralist and ideologue. Even when describing the
material causes of the plight of the working classes, he
displays an intense distaste for their manners and habits. Their wretchedness he finds "loathsome" and their
habits "gross"; they are inclined not only to thriftless-
ness but also to dissipation, and the two vices go hand in
hand. Soon Kay is blaming the poor themselves for
their condition, and shows no trace of his awareness of
circumstances beyond their control. In a revealing pas-
sage, he depicts the inhabitants of the slums as "denying themselves the comforts of life, in order that they
may wallow in the unrestrained license of animal appetite." This moralism, in turn, is powerfully reinforced
by the doctrines of political economy when Kay turns to
a discussion of wages, unemployment, and the poor law.
He takes up that subject with the flat assertion that the
wages earned by workers in the cotton industry would
be enough to provide them with all that they need if

only they were not "too often consumed by vice and *improvidence.*" With that phrase, Kay introduces a theme that pervades the rest of the pamphlet: the indissoluble links between "indigence, improvidence, idleness, and vice." The litany recurs in various forms, identifying the moral turpitude of the working class as the root cause of their poverty: "indigence and vice," "idleness, improvidence, and moral deviations," "sloth or dissipation," and "selfish profligacy." As Kay sees it, this cluster of interconnected vices is being actively fostered by the calamitous poor law, which both rewards sloth and also encourages the poor to marry early and reproduce themselves with reckless abandon. Here, in the best Malthusian manner, concern about population growth fuses with Puritan disapproval of sexual activity. Using the familiar Victorian code words—licentiousness and sensuality—Kay expresses his disgust with the sexual habits of the working classes, infected by "the moral leprosy of vice."

On the conscious level Kay formally rejected any tendency to blame the poor for their condition. In a prefatory letter to the report he wrote: "Some prejudiced men, accustomed to examine only one side of the shield, are . . . eager to attribute all ills suffered by the poor, solely to their ignorance or moral deviations." On the contrary, he argued, the poor cannot be blamed, for they suffered "under the pressure of extraneous grievances," and even their bad habits might be traced to the "primary influence of the imperfect institutions of society on their character," and the "desperate straits of a perverted spirit battling with hunger and toil." [4] Al-

[4] James Kay, *The Moral and Physical Condition of the Working Classes Employed in the Cotton Manufacture in Manchester* (Manchester, 1969), p. 6.

though this disclaimer reflects a clear intellectual perception of the problem, it did not penetrate to the level of Kay's actual attitudes and sentiments. He did, however, find it necessary to depict education as a means of improving a defective environment for which the poor were not responsible. But this was only a surface resolution of a deep ambivalence, for he continued to think and act as if the poor were individually responsible for their overall behavior.

Another factor which blunted Kay's initial awareness of the pressure of material circumstances in shaping the condition of the working classes was his faith in the intrinsic beneficence of unrestricted commerce. This faith receives striking expression in the pamphlet when, immediately after his devastating account of the woes of Manchester, Kay provides a lyrical paean to the city as a monument to "the power and dignity of man." Contemplating the warehouses and factories of Manchester, he rejoices at the natural tendency of commerce to minister to "the happiness of a favoured race." Taking this as his premise, he proceeds syllogistically to dismiss the notion that there might be a causal connection between the economic system and the ills which he has described so graphically: "A system which promotes the advance of civilization, and diffuses it over the world . . . cannot be inconsistent with the happiness of the *great mass of the people*." In fact, he tells us that one of his purposes in exposing the condition of the lower orders is to show that "the evils affecting them result *from foreign and accidental causes*." Chief among such causes are restrictions on trade, especially the corn laws. With the repeal of such noxious legislation, the beneficent and civilizing energy of commerce will be liberated, and men of good will can then get on with the job of correcting momentary defects and building the good society.

From this moral and ideological perspective Kay turns to popular education as the key to the solution of the problems posed by the condition of the working classes of Manchester. With "a virtuous population engaged in free trade," England would move forward. As a first step toward securing such a population Kay recommends the denial of relief to those whose poverty is the result of "dissipation, idleness, and willful imprudence," and the granting of relief to those who have demonstrated a readiness to overcome their deficiencies. Visitors should seek out the deserving poor and instruct them in thrift and domestic economy, thereby enabling them to understand that every laborer is the "surest architect of his own fortune." And there is no point in limiting such instruction to applicants for relief. The working classes as a whole are desperately in need of education. This is the burden of the rest of Kay's pamphlet: education must be the cornerstone of public policy in dealing with the working classes. He calls for increased religious instruction in order to raise the moral level of the masses in the large towns, and praises voluntary efforts already undertaken in Manchester and other urban areas. He describes the work of infant schools in other countries and expresses the hope that the government will furnish enough funds so that a "general system of education" can be provided for all of the children of the poor, who will be "rescued from ignorance."

In the course of the pamphlet, a second theme emerges and takes its place at the center of Kay's social and educational thought. Increasingly, he perceives the working classes not only as potential paupers but also as a threat to the social and political order. This threat too must be met by education. In his account of the worst section of Manchester, Kay describes a "turbulent population" which has been "misled" by intriguers and demagogues. He notes that "political desperadoes have ever loved to tempt this population to the hazards of the swindling game of revolution," and depicts all working-class agitation as the result of an unfortunate misunderstanding based on ignorance of the relevant facts and principles. In this vein, a few years later, he was to dismiss the Chartist leaders as "ignorant" and "unprincipled," "unscrupulous men" taking advantage of the "ignorance, discontent, and suffering of the mass." Given this conception of the causes of working-class agitation, Kay logically concludes that only education can enable the working classes to understand their "true interests" and reject the spurious arguments of the radicals. "The ascertained truths of political science should be early taught to the working classes, and *correct* political information should be constantly and industriously disseminated among them." In 1839, with the Chartists in the foreground, Kay was to put even more stress on the stabilizing function of popular education. The children of the poor had to be taught "to perceive their true relation to other classes of society." Education must "afford the labourer a clear view of his social position— its duties, its difficulties and rewards." The poor must understand "how their interests are inseparable from those of the other orders of society."

By the end of the pamphlet Kay has left the stench and disease of Manchester behind him and has moved into a purer realm, where popular education appears as the instrument of redemption. He calls for "a system of national education so extensive and liberal as to supply the wants of the whole labouring population."

II

Kay-Shuttleworth's outlook reflected his position in early Victorian society and culture. Three aspects of his situation were especially important. First of all, his basic attitudes and values corresponded quite closely to the views of the provincial bourgeoisie from which he had sprung. Secondly, he was imbued with a liberalism which expressed middle-class aspirations in opposition to the traditional toryism of the landed classes. Thirdly, the cast of his mind and the temper of his policies bear the imprint of the new administrative elite, of which he was a distinguished representative. Exercising a pervasive influence in all of these settings was the omnipresent force of utilitarianism and evangelical Christianity.

The social philosophy of the provincial bourgeoisie of early Victorian England had been hammered out on the anvil of the poor law issue during the period of continual debate that began in the late eighteenth century.[5] Their basic attitudes were a direct reflex of their social position. They expected workingmen to take orders, work hard, and play their customary roles; they viewed with alarm any symptoms of working-class indolence, indiscipline, or subversion. But these general attitudes—inherent in the relations of any master class to its servants—took on a particular form in the historical circumstances that prevailed in England in the generation before 1834, when the propertied classes became obsessed with the problem of the poor in a

[5] See J. R. Poynter, *Society and Pauperism: English Ideas on Poor Relief 1795-1834* (London, 1969) and R. H. Tawney, *Religion and the Rise of Capitalism* (New York, 1926), pp. 253-273.

framework of concern about population growth and the existing system of poor relief. In this context, socially determined attitudes took on a more rigid and doctrinaire character. For centuries the propertied classes had looked down with disdain on the manners and morals of the multitude, and from time to time their Christian zeal had taken the form of a crusade to eliminate the vices of the lower orders. In the course of the eighteenth century slothfulness came to be perceived as the besetting sin of the working classes, who had not proved sufficiently responsive to the requirements of the Protestant ethic. This moralistic view of the poor, in turn, was intensified by the onset of Malthusian anxiety about excessive population growth. "Sensuality" now moved up on the roster of working-class vices. Poor relief was stigmatized as an incentive to indolence, immorality, and procreation without end. At the same time, the new science of political economy, preached by the philosophic radicals, emphasized the threat posed to the free labor market by the existing system of poor relief: if the economy was to function efficiently and contribute to the greatest happiness of the greatest number, the poor must be compelled by every available means, especially the threat of workhouse, to seek work. Thus, the moralism of Christianity combined with the scientistic dogmatism of utilitarianism and the traditional prejudices of the propertied classes to produce an exceptionally harsh view of the poor. The poor had the worst of all worlds, for on the one hand they were treated as mere components of the economic machinery, while on the other hand they were held personally responsible for the moral and intellectual deficiencies that had led them into pauperism.

As a result of the work of men like Edwin Chadwick,

a Benthamite intellectual and bureaucrat, this view of the poor was enacted into law with full rigor in the Poor Law Amendment Act of 1834.[6] Chadwick was named secretary to the Poor Law Commission established by the Act. His friend and admirer, Kay-Shuttleworth, became an Assistant Commissioner and assumed his new duties with great enthusiasm.

Before joining the new national bureaucracy, Kay-Shuttleworth was active in a movement which embodied the grim philosophy of 1834 in a somewhat more positive spirit. In the early 1830's the Provident Societies set out to deal with the problem of poverty locally in the industrial towns by providing relief to the deserving poor.[7] An elaborate system of visitors was established to make sure that the undeserving did not receive any bounty. Another task of the visitors was to encourage the poor to be provident and make regular deposits in savings accounts, and to instruct them in domestic economy. They were also to be taught to understand their function in society and the laws governing the economy. Although the movement did not accomplish much, the effort that went into it is a reminder of the strength of the middle-class faith in the moral and intellectual reform of the individual as the solution to poverty and any other ills that beset society. That creed rested on the evangelical faith in moral renewal and redemption, and the utilitarian confidence in the diffusion of knowledge.

These middle-class attitudes toward the poor were usually embedded in a broader ideology, whose primary

[6] See S. E. Finer, *The Life and Times of Sir Edwin Chadwick* (London, 1952).

[7] See Manchester and Salford District Provident Society, *Annual Reports* (Manchester, 1833–1836).

thrust was directed against the landed classes and their
Tory outlook. In this tradition, Kay-Shuttleworth perceived himself as the spokesman for the new and progressive world of commerce, which he contrasted with
the static and reactionary world of "feudality." Middle-
class liberals saw themselves as exponents of advanced
and enlightened views, opposed by squires and lords
of narrow vision. In the field of education, the Tory
gentry had been at first quite hostile to popular education, on the grounds that it would be a stimulus to discontent and unrest. By the 1830's, however, they had
come to the conclusion that some sort of mass education was necessary, and even desirable, provided that
it was kept under the control of the Church. But they
had come around to this view only rather grudgingly,
and they conceived of popular education in the essentially negative terms characteristic of the eighteenth-
century charity schools and their early nineteenth-century successors. Teaching was to concentrate primarily
on religion, with only a minimum of attention to secular
subjects. Habits of obedience and deference were to be
instilled as part of indoctrination in religion and morality. It was an educational policy which reflected the
static society of the village, where the gentry expected
and received habitual deference from their social in-
feriors. Middle-class liberals on the other hand were
developing an alternative view of society and school.
In principle, they rejected the pattern of unthinking
acquiescence in favor of a society in which workingmen,
provided with a good education, recognized the sound-
ness of the views held by their superiors and accepted
them freely and rationally. As Kay-Shuttleworth saw
things, the Tories hoped to keep workingmen in a state
of "unenterprising contentment, uninstructed reverence,

and unrepining submission," whereas the poor ought to be educated "without undermining their independence or teaching them habits of servility." This was the ideal of the progressive middle class of the expanding world of the early Victorian cities. It envisaged the creation of an energetic and intelligent class of workingmen, responsive to the leadership of their superiors.[8]

Although middle-class liberalism spoke in radical accents when denouncing "feudal" notions of society and education, it nevertheless retained many attitudes characteristic of the propertied classes as a whole, rural as well as urban. Thus, it assumed a basically fixed class structure, in which a man remained in the position into which he had been born and performed his assigned duties. Egalitarian and democratic values were quite foreign to the early Victorian middle classes. Furthermore, their social ideal encompassed a substantial element of paternalism, which reflected the older traditions of the countryside. The men who formed the Provident Societies, for example, took it for granted that the initiative for popular improvement must come from above, and that the lower orders would, of course, have to look to their betters for guidance. Working-class "independence" would be stimulated and cultivated by the propertied classes. Kay-Shuttleworth was very much in tune with this socially conservative outlook.

But early Victorian liberals could afford to take for granted the assumptions of a shared social conservatism, while concentrating on points that divided them from their Tory opponents. In the area of popular education liberal principles led to a much more activist policy. Pre-

[8] See Simon, *Studies*, ch. III; W. H. Burston, ed., *James Mill on Education* (Cambridge, 1969); E. Halévy, *The Growth of Philosophic Radicalism* (London, 1928), pp. 282–295.

cisely because the liberal consciously rejected the traditional Tory expectation of blind obedience from the
working classes, he was obliged, in principle, to advocate
the provision of a much more "substantial" education,
which would enable them to arrive freely and independently at their own conclusions. If they were to be "intelligent supporters of order," they would have to learn
more than the Catechism and the three R's. If they were
to understand the principles of political economy and
thus grasp "the true causes which determine their physical condition and regulate the distribution of wealth
among the several classes of society," they would require
highly trained teachers. Similarly, the sort of moral re-
generation that Kay-Shuttleworth had in mind could not
be accomplished without a vast improvement in the
existing structure of popular education. Thus, the liberal
rejection of the Tory model of society led naturally to
support for expanded and improved education for the
working classes.

Kay-Shuttleworth's version of the standard middle-
class liberal belief in popular education was appreciably
influenced by the fact that he was not based in a factory
or warehouse in Manchester, but in a government office
in London. The social attitudes of the Provident Societies assumed quite a different spirit when translated to
the purlieus of the new bureaucracy. Kay-Shuttleworth
shared a number of important traits with the expanding
corps of commissioners, assistant commissioners, and inspectors who took as their province the most urgent
social problems of early Victorian England—from the
poor law and the prison system to factories, public
health, and education.[9] First and foremost, they exem-

---

[9] D. Roberts, *Victorian Origins of the Welfare State* (New
Haven, 1960), chs. 5 and 6, and passim.

plify the well known paradox of men who were committed to laissez faire and individualism, and imbued with a distrust of the state, but who nevertheless advocated extensive governmental interference to deal with the problems that came to their attention and who presided over the construction of a new central administrative apparatus. One source of their paradoxical behavior (and of Kay-Shuttleworth's as well) was some form of Benthamite utilitarianism, for, as Halévy pointed out in a classic analysis, that doctrine included not only the belief in laissez faire policy for the economy but also the notion that in many important areas, such as criminal law, governmental interference was required in order to bring about an artificial identification of interests.[10] Although the inspectors as a whole cannot be classified as Benthamite in a formalistic sense, they shared the fundamental utilitarian faith that human affairs should be ordered rationally on a scientific basis. Provided that the economy was left pretty much to itself, as the principle of laissez faire required, they felt no hesitation—indeed, they were often rather zealous—about issuing orders to set things straight. Their rationalistic and positivistic predisposition to interfere was reinforced by their administrative situation, as bureaucrats faced with muddle, amateurishness, and vested interests in the provinces; and by their contact with the facts of social and economic life, which obviously were not ordered in accord with a pre-existing harmony and could not be expected to correct themselves automatically. Finally, they were so wedded to the belief in the importance of the moral and intellectual improvement of the individual that they welcomed governmental intervention in that area. All

[10] Halévy, *Philosophic Radicalism*, ch. I; Finer, *Sir Edwin Chadwick*, ch. III.

of these men, regardless of their special field of interest, shared a faith in the reforming power of education. Among this group it fell to Kay-Shuttleworth to preside over the expansion of governmental activity into the area that they all agreed was of supreme importance.

The faith in education which characterized Kay-Shuttleworth and the new officialdom had been nurtured by the combined force of utilitarian rationalism and evangelical Christianity. If only the individual could be instructed in scientific knowledge and sound moral and political principles, unlimited progress would inevitably follow. The moral and intellectual improvement of the individual was accepted as a self-evident value by Victorians of all classes and shades of opinion. By virtue of his situation, Kay-Shuttleworth embraced that faith with somewhat more zeal and was able to make a strenuous effort to put it into practice.

III

When Kay-Shuttleworth took office in 1839, he soon found that he would have to work within the existing framework óf popular education and that a truly national system was quite out of the question. The education of the working classes was in the hands of two religious societies, Anglican and Nonconformist, which had been active for over a quarter of a century: the National Society for the Promotion of the Education of the Poor in the Principles of the Established Church and the British and Foreign School Society. Since 1833 the national government had been providing an annual grant of £20,000 to support the building of schools by the two groups. Although they accepted this money, both Anglicans and Nonconformists were suspicious of governmental intervention; the former feared a threat to their predominance, the latter feared that Anglican educational supremacy would be perpetuated. The "religious difficulty," as it came to be called, delayed the development of a state-supported system of popular education. Even in order to create a governmental agency in this sensitive area, it had been necessary to act through an Order in Council, which did not require prior parliamentary approval. The resulting Committee of Council on Education was an awkward body confronting a formidable array of vested interests, in no mood to be disturbed.[11]

The National Society was by far the more important of the two societies, both in the number of schools operating under its auspices and in the political influence that it exercised in Parliament. Almost immediately after the creation of the new Education Committee, the Tory-Anglican Establishment provided Kay-Shuttleworth with a forceful display of its power. In one of its first Minutes, the Committee had announced that it intended to erect a Normal School, which would be "under the direction of the State, and not placed under the management of a voluntary society"; that all future grants would be contingent on the acceptance of inspection; and that grants would not necessarily be limited to the two societies. The proposal for a Normal School drew a storm of criticism from Churchmen and was hastily withdrawn, but without quieting the opposition that had developed in the House of Commons. A motion to dissolve the Education Committee lost by only five votes. The annual grant

---

[11] See A. S. Bishop, *The Rise of a Central Authority for English Education* (Cambridge, 1971), chs. 1–3; Hurt, *Education in Evolution,* pp. 11–32; M. Sturt, *The Education of the People* (London, 1967), chs. 1–4; Smith, *Life and Work,* ch. 3.

passed by only two votes. Thus, at the very outset, the
forces of the Church had almost destroyed the fragile
enterprise that Kay-Shuttleworth had been called upon
to head. Moreover, as soon as he moved to implement
the new policy of inspection, he found that his opponents were bent on reducing its effect to a minimum.
The National Society extracted as many concessions as
possible before agreeing to a system of inspection a year
later. Under the agreement the Archbishops were given
the right to nominate candidates for the post of inspector
of Church schools and to approve appointments; they
were to issue instructions to the inspectors on religious
teaching and were to receive copies of the inspectors'
reports. Even after agreement was reached, difficulties
remained: the first inspector refused to address his reports to the Committee, and had to be compelled to
do so.[12]

After this encounter with the Church during his first
year in office, Kay-Shuttleworth was acutely conscious of
the need to compromise and to conciliate his opponents.
As a result of his patience and shrewdness, however, in
just a few years the National Society had come to accept
a system of inspection and control that went far beyond
the mild proposals that had aroused such opposition in
1839. The heart of his policy was embodied in the famous
Minutes of 1846.[13] He adopted a number of interlocking
measures which were intended to raise the level of teaching while increasing the flow of government funds into
the schools. In exchange for the money the schools acqui-
esced in an elaborate apparatus of supervision directed

[12] Smith, *Life and Work*, pp. 82–103; N. Gash, *Reaction and Reconstruction in English Politics* (Oxford, 1965), pp. 76–91.
[13] Smith, *Life and Work*, pp. 162–174; Hurt, *Education in Evolution*, ch. 4; A. Tropp, *The School Teachers* (London, 1957), ch. 2.

from the center by the Education Committee. Kay-Shuttleworth operated the system with bureaucratic energy and infused it with his consuming faith in education.

At the core of Kay-Shuttleworth's scheme was a system of pupil-teachers, to replace the monitors who had been so prominent in the schools of both religious societies from the very beginning. Although the monitorial system was pretty well discredited by the 1840's, no alternative had emerged. Kay-Shuttleworth's plan was designed to provide one. His idea was to recruit the best pupils from the existing schools and keep them on there as pupil-teachers from age thirteen to eighteen. During this period they would be supported by a government stipend. While performing their teaching duties, they would receive an hour and a half of instruction daily from the master in charge of the school. Thus, the untrained monitors would be replaced by selected pupil-teachers who would be participating in a regular instructional program. The new pupil-teacher system, in turn, was to be closely tied in with a government-sponsored expansion of the normal schools operated by the religious societies. At the age of eighteen, the best of the pupil-teachers would be given scholarships to the training colleges. Students completing the course were to take an examination set by the government. Successful candidates were certified. Moreover, the certification system was then extended to practicing teachers who had not received normal school training; they could acquire certification by taking an examination. With these measures Kay-Shuttleworth hoped to ensure a steady flow of well trained teachers into the elementary schools. He hoped to keep them there by a number of financial incentives.

Kay-Shuttleworth wanted his certificated teachers to be well paid. In the 1846 Minutes, he made an ambitious attempt to set minimum salaries that were well above the prevailing scale. Certificated teachers were to receive a stipend directly from the government. Schools hiring such a teacher were required to pay him a salary amounting to at least twice the government grant. They were also required to provide the teacher with a house rent free. Upon retirement, certificated teachers would be eligible for a government pension. Through such measures, Kay-Shuttleworth hoped not only to provide financial incentives that would be helpful in recruitment but also to raise the status of the elementary school teacher.

Kay-Shuttleworth had found ways of pouring government money into elementary education on a much larger scale than before: stipends to pupil-teachers, scholarships for students in the training colleges, salary grants and pensions to certificated teachers. In addition, the government also paid grants to teachers who were supervising pupil-teachers and to the training colleges based on the number of scholarship students enrolled. Thus he had brought about a fundamental change in the nature and extent of government support for elementary education. The Education Committee had moved far beyond the era of building grants. The big step having been taken under Kay-Shuttleworth's leadership, only a few years after his retirement the Committee moved on to the provision of direct capitation grants to the schools. By 1859, there were over 15,000 pupil-teachers and just under 7,000 certificated teachers. Moreover, the amount of government money expended in support of popular education had increased enormously, from £100,000 in 1846, to over £800,000 in 1859.

The 1846 Minutes also enabled Kay to increase the influence and control that might be exercised from Lon-

don over schools that had jealously guarded their independence of central authority for so long. Grants were
made only to pupil-teachers and teachers who were working in schools that had passed their annual inspection.
The schools had no choice but to conform to standards
laid down by the Education Committee. Similarly, the
Committee determined the content of the certification
examinations, which affected curriculum in the normal
schools, which also were subject to inspection. No longer
could the schools operated by the religious societies do
pretty much as they chose. Henceforth they were to be
responsive to public policy, as laid down by the Education Committee and enforced by inspectors. The inspectorate was a standard Benthamite device, in use since
1833 in the enforcement of factory legislation. But the
education inspectorate started out on a very small scale,
with only two inspectors to cover some seven hundred
schools in England and Wales. In 1843 Kay-Shuttleworth
reorganized and extended the system. There were to be
five inspectors for Church-of-England schools, one for
normal schools, and one for the schools of the British
and Foreign School Society. Since the new inspectors had
no special knowledge of elementary education, Kay-Shuttleworth's letters to them provided a sort of on the job
training by correspondence. He discussed the most minute details of the operation of the school, and sent them
reading material including tracts on the Pestalozzian
system. Even when Kay-Shuttleworth took a holiday in
the Lake District, in search of "rest and relaxation" in
the summer of 1844, he managed to write almost daily
letters to his inspectors. In return, he received not only
regular reports from them but also their rough note
journals. He was relentless in his pursuit of the best
possible system of popular education. But Kay-Shuttle-

worth was unable to sustain this frenetic pace. In 1849 he collapsed from overwork and was forced to retire.[14]

IV

What did Kay-Shuttleworth accomplish during his ten years as secretary of the Education Committee? In the short run, he achieved a striking success, despite widespread opposition, in creating a system of governmental support and supervision of popular education. In the long run, his achievement was less substantial, especially when viewed in the light of what he hoped for. An historical assessment of Kay-Shuttleworth's life and work cannot be confined to a consideration of specific consequences, however. It must also take account of the quality and intensity of his faith in education and his tireless devotion to the cause. We shall consider first the long-term results of his work.

Kay-Shuttleworth's high hopes, rooted in early Victorian utopianism and in the hubris of the activist administrator, fell far short of realization for historical circumstances made it impossible to achieve the superior system of popular education of which he dreamed. Although he constructed a solid administrative edifice, no amount of bureaucratic supervision could overcome the effect of two limiting conditions which he had no choice but to accept. First of all, a segregated system of education for the lower orders was bound to be inferior from the very outset. The implications of the decision to equate popular education with education for the poor, which Kay-Shuttleworth took for granted, were inescapable. In the second

14 Smith, *Life and Work,* ch. 7.

place, the particular institutions which he had been obliged to work with were, after all, essentially charity schools for the poor and they retained that character. The chief practical effect of Kay-Shuttleworth's policies was a great increase in the subsidy which the central government provided to the denominational schools, the vast majority of which were Anglican, operated by men who had opposed him in the 1840's and who conceived of popular education within the narrow framework of religious instruction and social control. Even when prodded by diligent inspectors, such schools were able to attain only minimal standards.

Kay-Shuttleworth's ambitious plans were bound to be undermined by the attitude of the mid-Victorian middle classes, who took a much narrower view of the nature and scope of popular education. As soon as the implications of the 1846 Minutes became clear in the 1850's, the new system ran into very heavy criticism.[15] Although specific complaints varied, the extent of the opposition was unmistakable. The sharp increase in expenditure was, of course, disturbing in and of itself. And the trend was particularly disquieting to Nonconformists, who saw most of the state funds going to Church schools. Criticism of popular education went even deeper than this. What troubled the middle classes was the fact that the schools seemed bent on providing the poor with a much better education than they needed and deserved. School teachers, recruited from the working classes, were being over-educated for their station, were over-paid, and were acquiring exaggerated notions of their worth and status in society. These teachers, it was complained, took a great deal more interest in providing advanced instruc-

[15] Tropp, *The School Teachers*, ch. 5.

tion to their better pupils than in teaching the funda-
mentals to the great majority. The middle-class reaction
to Kay-Shuttleworth's policies was plain: working-class
education should be cheaper and less ambitious. It was
partly in response to this body of opinion that Robert
Lowe, Vice-President of the Committee of Council on
Education, introduced the Revised Code.[16] The Code
reduced expenditure on popular education by replacing
the various stipends and grants with a single payment
made directly to the schools. It established the system of
"payment by results," whereby the amount of the grant
was based on pupils' success in an examination in the
three R's administered by government inspectors. Kay-
Shuttleworth emerged from retirement to denounce the
Code and defend the 1846 Minutes.

The Revised Code provides a convenient touchstone
for an assessment of Kay-Shuttleworth's policies. In the
older histories of education it was treated as a regressive
action which arrested the progressive line of development
initiated by the 1846 Minutes.[17] The contrast between

[16] See Bishop, *Rise of a Central Authority*, ch. 4. In 1858 was
published an abstract of the policies and regulations contained in
Minutes which had been issued by the Education Committee. Re-
issued in a different format in 1860, the regulations came to be
known as "The Original Code." Lowe's "Revised Code" was the
first revision. In 1857, the post of Vice-President of the Committee
of Council on Education was created. Robert Lowe became Vice-
President in 1859 and served until 1864. In the next few years, he
achieved some notoriety as a ferocious opponent of even a moderate
extension of the franchise to the working classes. See A. Briggs,
Victorian People (London, 1954), ch. 9.

[17] See, for example, Barnard, *History of English Education*, pp.
111–114. For a revisionist view which attempts to swing the balance
in Lowe's favor, see Hurt, *Education in Evolution*, pp. 93, 208, 220.
See also B. Simon, *Education and the Labour Movement, 1870–1920*
(London, 1965), pp. 115–118, for a suggestive discussion of the
problem.

the two is certainly important and we shall consider it shortly. On the other hand, it would be a mistake to imply that Robert Lowe single-handedly reversed the course set in 1846. In fact, the Revised Code merely dramatized developments which were already inherent in the system of popular education and its relationship to Victorian society. Socially segregated educational institutions in an inegalitarian society were bound to be operated on the cheap. Although Kay-Shuttleworth's idealism had momentarily produced a rather ambitious scheme, it could not prevail in the face of countervailing social forces. Sooner or later popular education would reach the level determined by the interests and values of the propertied classes.

The fact that Kay-Shuttleworth's policies aroused opposition which culminated in the Revised Code should not be taken solely as an indication of his failure. It also symbolizes the quality that raised him above the level of an ordinary administrator: the extent to which he transcended the limits imposed by the class to which he belonged. Although his outlook reflected middle-class values and ideology, his policies—and even more his aspirations —went well beyond what the middle classes considered a proper education for the working classes. He commands our respect because he took seriously the early Victorian faith in education and in the moral and intellectual improvement of the individual. Despite his belief in laissez faire, he tried to enlist the resources of the national government in behalf of the official goals of the community. He set himself apart from a middle class which combined a sincere devotion to the ideal of social and intellectual progress with a more fundamental determination to keep the working classes in their traditional state of subordination. Kay-Shuttleworth, to be sure, was

equally wedded to the existing class structure and conceived of education as a means of enabling workingmen
to understand their place in society. But he did not permit these social attitudes to shut out a broader vision of
what popular education might achieve. And he supported that vision with a bold program for the recruitment, training, and payment of teachers.

Kay-Shuttleworth's distinctive qualities stand out
clearly in contrast to Robert Lowe—a contrast all the
more instructive because the two men had so much in
common. Both were utilitarians who believed in a static
class structure and a laissez faire economy. Lowe, however, subscribed to a narrowly middle-class version of
nineteenth-century liberalism, whereas Kay-Shuttleworth
had responded to the universal values and aspirations
at its core.

Lowe's defense of the Revised Code echoed much of
the middle-class criticism of the 1850's. While denying
the charge that the Code was "degrading education" by
concentrating primarily on the three R's, he made it
plain that he saw no point in trying to teach much more:
"We do not object to any amount of learning; the only
question is, how much of that knowledge ought we to
pay for?" His answer came in the form of a rhetorical
question: since the poor man's child leaves school at age
eleven, is it not enough to teach him simply to read,
write, and cipher? He then reminded the House of Commons that they were, after all, discussing the sort of
education that should be provided for children whose
parents were unable to pay for it. "We do not profess
to give these children an education that will raise them
above their station and business in life." Presumably the
1846 Minutes had shown such a tendency, especially in
the matter of the recruitment and payment of elementary

school teachers. Lowe took pride in the fact that these "overeducated men" had been deprived of the grants that they had been receiving from the government. He rebuked Kay-Shuttleworth for having suggested that teachers had a right to "repose and freedom from anxiety," and should not be "worked like a horse on a gin mill." He decried the notion that they should be maintained in the "social status" created by the 1846 Minutes.[18]

The Revised Code provided a perfect foil for Kay-Shuttleworth, and he seized the occasion to reaffirm his more exalted conceptions of what popular education ought to be. He defended teachers against the charge that they were too highly instructed. He denounced the policies which he saw as the crux of the new Code: "The children of parents supported by manual labour in Great Britain shall have a less costly education—all classes of their teachers shall be trained at less expense, shall be worse paid, and be fewer in number than they are now—instruction shall be chiefly technical and quite elementary." In principle, Kay-Shuttleworth stood for "quality education" for all. He insisted that the nation should not regard the mass of the people as mere beasts of burden, but should instead take an active interest in their "intelligence, inventive capacity, morality, and fitness for the duties of freemen and citizens." Hence their education should not be limited to the three R's. Although Kay-Shuttleworth had no more interest than Lowe in educating the poor "above their station," he had been carried away by his faith in the redemptive power of education. Having absorbed the optimistic ra-

[18] *Hansard's Parliamentary Debates.* Third Series, Vol. CLXV (1862), c. 211–213, 237–238.

tionalism of the early nineteenth century, he believed
that within every man lie resources of rationality that
ought to be cultivated. His fidelity to that principle set
him apart from men like Lowe.

V

Kay-Shuttleworth's belief in education was not unique
to England, of course, but was central to European and
American liberalism. In the reformist and often utopian
atmosphere of the 1830's and 1840's, that faith quickened
and assumed diverse forms, while maintaining the underlying unity of outlook that was rooted in the shared
culture of the Enlightenment. Kay-Shuttleworth's ideas
should be seen in this broader historical framework. A
glance at Horace Mann, his American counterpart, may
serve to highlight some of the distinctive aspects of Kay's
thought while reminding us of how much of his outlook
was widely shared. Their careers paralleled each other,
chronologically and otherwise. A few years older than
Kay-Shuttleworth, Mann came to education from the
law. From 1837 to 1848, he served as secretary of the
newly created Massachusetts Board of Education. Like
Kay-Shuttleworth, he extolled the virtues of popular education, but in very different spirit—optimistic, democratic, egalitarian—which reflected the aspirations of a
nation that took pride in having escaped the class-ridden
values of Europe.[19]
Since the differences between Kay-Shuttleworth and
Mann are so conspicuous, the points of similarity are all

[19] See L. A. Cremin, ed., *The Republic and the School: Horace
Mann on the Education of Free Men* (New York, 1957); J. Messerli,
Horace Mann: A Biography (New York, 1972).

the more noteworthy. Like Kay-Shuttleworth, for example, Mann saw popular education as a barrier against social unrest and disorder. In language strikingly similar to Kay-Shuttleworth's, Mann argued that unless children were provided with a proper education, they might develop into "incendiaries and madmen to destroy property and life, and to invade and pollute the sanctuaries of society." In the same vein, he decried the consequences of a failure to educate the people: "poverty and destitution . . . the scourges of violence and misrule . . . the heart-destroying corruptions of licentiousness and debauchery, . . . political profligacy and legalized perfidy." [20] Like Kay-Shuttleworth, Mann emphasized the importance of moral instruction, based on the principles of a non-sectarian, non-Fundamentalist Protestantism. In America, as in England, Christian values complemented the educational influence of the Enlightenment. In Mann, as in Kay-Shuttleworth, we find anxiety about the danger posed by the immorality and ignorance of the mass of the people.

While Mann saw education as a means of defense against poverty and radicalism, however, this was only incidental to his broader vision of popular education as a means of building an open society characterized by genuine equality of opportunity. He saw education as the "great equalizer of the conditions of men—the balance-wheel of the social machinery," and hoped that education would "obliterate factitious distinctions in society." Mann was concerned about the "fatal extremes of overgrown wealth and desperate poverty," whereas Kay-Shuttleworth was preoccupied only with the latter, for which he blamed the poor themselves. Like Kay-Shuttleworth,

[20] Cremin, *The Republic and the School*, pp. 75–76.

Mann argued that education would foster independence and combat servility. But Mann was worried about the servility of labor that resulted from the domination of capital, whereas Kay-Shuttleworth equated servility with feudal forms of domination alone. Thus, although Kay-Shuttleworth and Mann started from many of the assumptions common to early nineteenth century liberalism, they arrived at conceptions of popular education that reflected the profound differences between English and American society. Mann hoped that education would solve the problem of poverty and create a more egalitarian society by enabling the poor not merely to escape pauperism but to acquire property, and in effect to enter the middle class. "Property and labor, in different classes, are essentially antagonistic, but property and labor in the same class are essentially fraternal." The common school would bring together children from varied backgrounds, provide them with a liberal education, and enlarge "the cultivated class." [21] The end product, Mann was sure, would be a society of free men, not divided by artificial distinctions of class or wealth.

The comparison to Mann underlines the class character of Kay-Shuttleworth's educational policies. He took it for granted that popular education meant a separate system for the poor, whereas Mann wanted above all to make sure that the common school did not become a mere pauper school. For Kay-Shuttleworth, the inculcation of common values meant helping the working classes to see themselves and society from a middle-class point of view, whereas Mann hoped that a common educational experience and development of shared democratic values would reduce social differences to a minimum.

[21] *Ibid.*, pp. 86–87.

Kay-Shuttleworth's idealism was hobbled not only by his social presuppositions but also by the social and institutional structure which had produced those social attitudes in the first place. He contributed to the creation of a segregated system of education which twentieth-century reformers have been striving to transform, often with an admiring glance at the American common school.

It would be misleading to leave the matter there, however, with an apparent sigh of gratitude to a beneficent Providence for ordering things so well in the United States. Kay-Shuttleworth's inability to actualize his ideals was the consequence of tensions and contradictions inherent in liberalism in all its manifestations, including the American. The liberal tradition which took shape in the course of the eighteenth century combined an aspiration to foster the moral and intellectual development of the individual with a commitment to a social and economic system which made it difficult to achieve that ideal in its full universality. The class structure posed an insuperable obstacle. In America, the dilemma was concealed, as in the thought of Horace Mann, by the proclamation of an egalitarian ethos which formally exorcised the demon of class, and by the absence of a rigid class system of the European type. Yet in America as in Europe liberal ideals have had little practical effect when they ran counter to patterns determined by the social and economic structure.

In twentieth-century England the mantle of liberalism has passed to the Labour Party and the socialists. Educational reformers on the Left have shed the social presuppositions which limited the scope of Kay-Shuttleworth's work, and their main target has been the class-ridden educational system which he helped to build. Yet even these men have been unable to resolve the dilemma inherent in liberalism: the incapacity of institutional reform to achieve goals which are incompatible with the class structure. In fact, they have been caught up in one of the more ironic episodes of recent social history. Educational reformers devoted to equality of opportunity—including men of the stature of R. H. Tawney—have played an important part in constructing an educational system which serves as the chief processing agent in a highly stratified and inegalitarian society.[22] To point this out is not to depreciate their efforts or their principles. But it does serve as a reminder that Kay-Shuttleworth's failure to fulfill his hopes was the consequence not only of his middle-class attitudes but also of the fact that all educational reformers—even those who are determined to eliminate the factitious influence of class from the pure realm of the school room—have to contend with an immensely stubborn substructure of social reality, which offers glacial resistance to reform.

From the perspective of the 1970's, then, one is struck not so much by Kay-Shuttleworth's failure to achieve his ambitious goals as by the character of his ideals and his devotion to them. Burdened by a particularly harsh version of bourgeois liberalism, he transcended his social and ideological background and reached out to the values at the heart of the liberal tradition. In that spirit he served the cause of popular education with distinc-

---

[22] For some of the complex developments embraced in this generalization, see O. Banks, *Parity and Prestige in English Secondary Education* (London, 1955); D. Marsden and B. Jackson, *Education and the Working Class* (Harmondsworth, 1966); J. Ford, *Social Class and the Comprehensive School* (London, 1969); B. Simon, "Classification and Streaming: A Study of Grouping in English Schools, 1860–1960," in P. Nash, ed., *History and Education* (New York, 1970).

tion, albeit within the limits imposed by his historical situation.

SUGGESTIONS FOR FURTHER READING

A superb bibliography of Kay-Shuttleworth's writings has been compiled by B. C. Bloomfield, "Sir James Phillips Kay-Shuttleworth (1804–1877): A Trial Bibliography," *British Journal of Educational Studies,* Vol. IX, No. 2 (1961), and "Addendum," *ibid.,* Vol. X, No. 1 (1961). Two useful collections of his writings are *Four Periods of Public Education as Reviewed in 1832–1839–1846–1862 in Papers by Sir James Kay-Shuttleworth, Bart.* (London, 1862), and *Thoughts and Suggestions on Certain Social Problems Contained Chiefly in Addresses to Meetings of Workmen in Lancashire* (London, 1873). Two of Kay-Shuttleworth's pamphlets are now available in reprints: *The Moral and Physical Condition of the Working Classes Employed in the Cotton Manufacture in Manchester* (Manchester, 1969) and *Memorandum on Popular Education* (London, 1969). His autobiography, written in 1877, has been edited by B. C. Bloomfield, *The Autobiography of Sir James Kay-Shuttleworth* (London, 1964).

Frank Smith, *The Life and Work of Sir James Kay-Shuttleworth* (London, 1923), is a solid biography. A. S. Bishop, *The Rise of a Central Authority for English Education* (Cambridge, 1971), has an excellent chapter on Kay-Shuttleworth's work. John Hurt, *Education in Evolution: Church, State, Society and Popular Education, 1800–1870* (London, 1971), deals extensively with Kay-Shuttleworth and advances a more favorable interpretation of Lowe and the Revised Code. Of particular value for an understanding of the 1846 Minutes is Asher

Tropp, *The School Teachers: the Growth of the Teaching Profession in England from 1800 to the Present* (London, 1957). Brian Simon, *Studies in the History of Education, 1780–1870* (London, 1960), includes a close analysis of Kay-Shuttleworth's social and educational thought. Richard Johnson, "Educational Policy and Social Control in Early Victorian England," *Past and Present,* No. 49 (1970), deals suggestively with Kay-Shuttleworth from the point of view indicated in the title. For a perceptive essay on Kay-Shuttleworth, see A. V. Judges, *Pioneers of English Education* (London, 1970). Alexander M. Ross, "Kay-Shuttleworth and the Training of Teachers for Pauper Schools," *British Journal of Educational Studies* Vol. XV (1967), describes his educational activity as Assistant Poor Law Commissioner. An interesting article on Kay-Shuttleworth's successor is A. S. Bishop, "Ralph Lingen, Secretary to the Education Department 1849–1870," *ibid.,* Vol. XVI (1968). For a fine account of Kay-Shuttleworth as a representative figure in the new early Victorian administrative elite, see David Roberts, *The Victorian Origins of the Welfare State* (New Haven, 1960). Other useful studies of Kay-Shuttleworth will be found in H. M. Pollard, *Pioneers of Popular Education, 1760–1850* (London, 1956), and W. A. C. Stewart and W. P. McCann, *The Educational Innovators, 1750–1880* (London, 1967).

Asa Briggs, "The Study of the History of Education," *History of Education,* Vol. I (1972), is an excellent introduction to the history of education in modern England. J. W. Adamson, *English Education, 1789–1902* (Cambridge, 1930), and H. C. Barnard, *A History of English Education from 1760* (London, 1961), provide general accounts of the development of English education in the nineteenth century. For popular education, see M. Sturt,

The Education of the People (London, 1967); F. Smith,
A History of English Elementary Education, 1760–1902
(London, 1931); C. Birchenough, *History of Elementary
Education* (London, 1938); and D. Wardle, *English Pop-
ular Education, 1780–1970* (Cambridge, 1970), a brief
survey. The religious rivalries with which Kay-Shuttle-
worth had to contend are examined in G. F. A. Best,
"The Religious Difficulties of National Education in
England," *Cambridge Historical Journal,* Vol. XII (1956).
H. Burgess, *Enterprise in Education* (London, 1958),
covers the work of the National Society, while H. B.
Binns, *A Century of Education, 1808–1908* (London,
1908), deals with its rival, the British and Foreign School
Society. For a study of education in a single city, see
D. Wardle, *Education and Society in Nineteenth Century
Nottingham* (Cambridge, 1971). Also useful are E. L.
Edmonds, *The School Inspector* (London, 1962); R. W.
Rich, *The Training of Teachers in England and Wales
during the Nineteenth Century* (London, 1933); A. Silver,
The Concept of Popular Education (London, 1965);
J. M. Goldstrom, *The Social Content of Education*
(Shannon, 1972). An excellent over-view is G. Sutherland,
Elementary Education in the Nineteenth Century (Lon-
don, 1971).

There are a number of anthologies of primary sources
which will be of interest to the student of the history of
popular education. Directly concerned with that topic is
J. M. Goldstrom, ed., *Education: Elementary Education
1780–1900* (Newton Abbot, 1972). Covering a broader
range of educational developments are J. S. Maclure, ed.,
Educational Documents: England and Wales, 1816–1967
(London, 1968), and P. H. J. H. Gosden, ed., *How They
Were Taught* (Oxford, 1969). A briefer collection is
E. Midwinter, ed., *Nineteenth Century Education* (New

York, 1970). For the ideas of men to the left of Kay-Shuttleworth, see B. Simon, ed., *The Radical Tradition in Education in Britain* (London, 1972), which includes selections from William Godwin and William Lovett among others; and J. F. C. Harrison, ed., *Utopianism and Education: Robert Owen and the Owenites* (New York, 1968).

1

The Moral and Physical Condition
of the Working Classes of
Manchester in 1832
(1832)

*This selection provides a full statement of the social phi-
losophy underlying Kay-Shuttleworth's approach to popular education. It also shows the development of the
conviction that education was the only remedy for the
ills afflicting the working classes, whom he encountered
as a young doctor in the slums of industrial Manchester.
Kay-Shuttleworth's classic study has been much admired
by social historians, among them Friedrich Engels who
drew on this "excellent pamphlet" in writing his* Condition of the English Working Class *in 1844.*

*When Kay-Shuttleworth published his collected papers
under the title* Four Periods of Public Education, *he
assigned this pamphlet to the first period, whose distinguishing characteristic was the failure of the central government to take any steps to mitigate the popular ignorance which he found so appalling.*

Self-knowledge, inculcated by the maxim of the ancient
philosopher, is a precept not less appropriate to societies

than to individuals. The physical and moral evils by which we are personally surrounded, may be more easily avoided when we are distinctly conscious of their existence; and the virtue and health of society may be preserved, with less difficulty, when we are acquainted with the sources of its errors and diseases.

The sensorium of the animal structure, to which converge the sensibilities of each organ, is endowed with a consciousness of every change in the sensations to which each member is liable; and few diseases are so subtle as to escape its delicate perceptive power. Pain thus reveals to us the existence of evils, which, unless arrested in their progress, might insidiously invade the source of vital action.

Society were well preserved, did a similar faculty preside, with an equal sensibility, over its constitution; making every order immediately conscious of the evils affecting any portion of the general mass, and thus rendering their removal equally necessary for the immediate ease, as it is for the ultimate welfare of the whole social system. The mutual dependence of the individual members of society and of its various orders, for the supply of their necessities and the gratification of their desires, is acknowledged, and it imperfectly compensates for the want of a faculty, resembling that pervading consciousness which presides over the animal economy. But a knowledge of the moral and physical evils oppressing one order of the community, is by these means slowly communicated to those which are remote; and general efforts are seldom made for the relief of partial ills, until they threaten to convulse the whole social constitution. . . .

The introduction into this country of a singularly malignant contagious malady, which, though it selects its victims from every order of society, is chiefly propagated amongst those whose health is depressed by disease, mental anxiety, or want of the comforts and conveniences of life, has directed public attention to an investigation of the state of the poor. In Manchester, Boards of Health were established, in each of the fourteen districts of Police, for the purpose of minutely inspecting the state of the houses and streets. These districts were divided into minute sections, to each of which two or more inspectors were appointed from among the most respectable inhabitants of the vicinity, and they were provided with tabular queries, applying to each particular house and street. Individual exceptions only exist, in which minute returns were not furnished to the Special Board: and as the investigation was prompted equally by the demands of benevolence, of personal security, and of the general welfare, the results may be esteemed as accurate as the nature of the investigation would permit. The other facts contained in this pamphlet have been obtained from the public offices of the town, or are the results of the author's personal observation.

The township of Manchester chiefly consists of dense masses of houses, inhabited by the population engaged in the great manufactories of the cotton trade. Some of the central divisions are occupied by warehouses and shops, and a few streets by the dwellings of some of the more wealthy inhabitants; but the opulent merchants chiefly reside in the country, and even the superior servants of their establishments inhabit the suburban townships. Manchester, properly so called, is chiefly inhabited by shopkeepers and the labouring classes. . . .[1]

---

[1] To the stranger, it is also necessary to observe, that the investigations on whose results the conclusions of this pamphlet are founded, were of necessity conducted *in the township of Manchester only;* and that the inhabitants of a great part of the adjacent town-

When this example is considered in connection with the unremitted labour of the whole population engaged in the various branches of the cotton manufacture, our wonder will be less excited by their fatal demoralisation. Prolonged and exhausting labour, continued from day to day, and from year to year, is not calculated to develop the intellectual or moral faculties of man. The dull routine of a ceaseless drudgery, in which the same mechanical process is incessantly repeated, resembles the torment of Sisyphus—the toil, like the rock, recoils perpetually on the wearied operative. The mind gathers neither stores nor strength from the constant extension and retraction of the same muscles. The intellect slumbers in supine inertness; but the grosser parts of our nature attain a rank development. To condemn man to such monotonous toil is, in some measure, to cultivate in him the habits of an animal. He becomes reckless. He disregards the distinguishing appetites and habits of his species. He neglects the comforts and delicacies of life. He lives in squalid wretchedness, on meagre food, and expends his superfluous gains in debauchery. . . .

The operatives are congregated in rooms and workshops during twelve hours in the day, in an enervating, heated atmosphere, which is frequently loaded with dust or filaments of cotton, or impure from constant respiration, or from other causes. They are engaged in an employment which absorbs their attention, and unremittingly employs their physical energies. They are drudges who watch the movements, and assist the operations, of a mighty material force, which toils with an energy ever

ships are in a condition superior to that described in these pages. The most respectable portion of the operative population has, we think, a tendency to avoid the central districts of Manchester, and to congregate in the suburban townships.

unconscious of fatigue. The persevering labour of the operative must rival the mathematical precision, the incessant motion, and the exhaustless power of the machine.

Hence, besides the negative results—the abstraction of moral and intellectual stimuli—the absence of variety—banishment from the grateful air and the cheering influences of light, the physical energies are impaired by toil, and imperfect nutrition. The artisan too seldom possesses sufficient moral dignity or intellectual or organic strength to resist the seductions of appetite. His wife and children, subjected to the same process, have little power to cheer his remaining moments of leisure. Domestic economy is neglected, domestic comforts are too frequently unknown. A meal of coarse food is hastily prepared, and devoured with precipitation. Home has little other relation to him than that of shelter—few pleasures are there—it chiefly presents to him a scene of physical exhaustion, from which he is glad to escape. His house is ill furnished, uncleanly, often ill ventilated—perhaps damp; his food, from want of forethought and domestic economy, is meagre and innutritious; he generally becomes debilitated and hypochondriacal, and, unless supported by principle, falls the victim of dissipation. In all these respects, it is grateful to add, that those among the operatives of the mills, who are employed *in the process of spinning,* and especially of fine spinning (who receive a high rate of wages and who are elevated on account of their skill), are more attentive to their domestic arrangements, have better furnished houses, are consequently more regular in their habits, and more observant of their duties than those engaged in other branches of the manufacture.

The other classes of artisans of whom we have spoken, are frequently subject to a disease, in which the sensibility of the stomach and bowels is morbidly excited; the alvine secretions are deranged, and the appetite impaired. Whilst this state continues, the patient loses flesh, his features are sharpened, the skin becomes sallow, or of the yellow hue which is observed in those who have suffered from the influence of tropical climates. The strength fails, the capacities of physical enjoyment are destroyed, and the paroxysms of corporeal suffering are aggravated by deep mental depression. We cannot wonder that the wretched victim of this disease, invited by those haunts of misery and crime the gin shop and the tavern, as he passes to his daily labour, should endeavour to cheat his suffering of a few moments, by the false excitement procured by ardent spirits; or that the exhausted artisan, driven by ennui and discomfort from his squalid home, should strive, in the delirious dreams of a continued debauch, to forget the remembrance of his reckless improvidence, of the destitution, hunger, and uninterrupted toil, which threaten to destroy the remaining energies of his enfeebled constitution. . . .

Predisposition to contagious disease is encouraged by everything which depresses the physical energies, amongst the principal of which agencies may be enumerated imperfect nutrition; exposure to cold and moisture, whether from inadequate shelter, or from want of clothing and fuel, or from dampness of the habitation; uncleanliness of the person, the street, and the abode; an atmosphere contaminated, whether from the want of ventilation, or from impure effluvia; extreme labour, and consequent physical exhaustion; intemperance; fear; anxiety; diarrhoea, and other diseases. The whole of these subjects could not be included in the investigation, though it originated in a desire to remove, as far as possible, those ills which depressed the health of the population. The list of inquiries to which the inspectors were requested to make tabular replies is placed in the appendix, for the purpose of enabling the reader to form his own opinion of the investigation from which the classified results are deduced.

The state of the streets powerfully affects the health of their inhabitants. Sporadic cases of typhus chiefly appear in those which are narrow, ill ventilated, unpaved, or which contain heaps of refuse, or stagnant pools. The confined air and noxious exhalations, which abound in such places, depress the health of the people, and on this account contagious diseases are also most rapidly propagated there. The operation of these causes is exceedingly promoted by their reflex influence on the manners. The houses, in such situations, are uncleanly, ill provided with furniture; an air of discomfort if not of squalid and loathsome wretchedness pervades them, they are often dilapidated, badly drained, damp: and the habits of their tenants are gross—they are ill fed, ill clothed, and uneconomical—at once spendthrifts and destitute—denying themselves the comforts of life, in order that they may wallow in the unrestrained licence of animal appetite. An intimate connection subsists, among the poor, between the cleanliness of the street and that of the house and person. Uneconomical habits and dissipation are almost inseparably allied; and they are so frequently connected with uncleanliness, that we cannot consider their concomitance as altogether accidental. The first step to recklessness may often be traced in a neglect of that self-respect, and of the love of domestic enjoyments, which are indicated by personal slovenliness, and discomfort of the habitation. Hence, the importance of providing by police regulations or general enactment, against those fertile sources alike of disease and demoralisation, presented by the gross neglect of the streets and habitations of the poor. When the health is depressed by the concurrence of these causes, contagious diseases spread with a fatal malignancy among the population subjected to their influence. The records of the Fever Hospital of Manchester prove that typhus *prevails almost exclusively* in such situations. . . .

The houses of the poor, especially throughout the whole of the Districts Nos. 1, 2, 3, 4, are too generally built back to back, having therefore only one outlet, no yard, no privy, and no receptacle of refuse. Consequently the narrow, unpaved streets, in which mud and water stagnate, become the common receptacles of offal and ordure. Often low, damp, ill-ventilated cellars exist beneath the houses; an improvement on which system consists in the erection of a stage over the first story, by which access is obtained to the second, and the house is inhabited by two separate families. More than one disgraceful example of this might be enumerated. The streets, in the districts where the poor reside, are generally unsewered, and the drainage is consequently superficial. The houses are often built with a total neglect of order, on the summit of natural irregularities of the surface, or on mounds left at the side of artificial excavations on the brick grounds, with which these parts of the town abound.

One nuisance frequently occurs in these districts of so noxious a character, that it ought, at the earliest period, to be suppressed by legal interference. The houses of the poor sometimes surround a common area, into which the doors and windows open at the back of the dwelling. Porkers, who feed pigs in the town, often contract with the inhabitants to pay some small sum for the rent of their area, which is immediately covered with pigstyes, and converted into a dung-heap and receptacle of the putrescent garbage, upon which the animals are fed, as also of the refuse which is now heedlessly flung into it from all the surrounding dwellings. The offensive odour which sometimes arises from these areas cannot be conceived.

There is no *Common* Slaughter-house in Manchester, and those which exist are chiefly situated in the narrowest and most filthy streets in the town. The drainage from these houses, deeply tinged with blood, and impregnated with other animal matters, frequently flows down the common surface drain of the street, and stagnates in the ruts and pools. Moreover, sometimes in the yards of these houses—from the want of a vigilant circumspection—offal is allowed to accumulate with the grossest neglect of decency and disregard to the health of the surrounding inhabitants. The attention of the commissioners of police cannot be too soon directed to the propriety of obtaining powers to erect a Common Slaughter-house on some vacant space, and to compel the butchers of the town to slaughter all animals killed in the township in the building thus provided.

The Districts Nos. 1, 2, 3, and 4, are inhabited by a turbulent population, which, rendered reckless by dissipation and want,—misled by the secret intrigues, and excited by the inflammatory harangues of demagogues, has frequently committed daring assaults on the liberty of the more peaceful portions of the working classes, and the most frightful devastations on the property of their masters. Machines have been broken, and factories gutted and burned at mid-day, and the riotous crowd has dispersed ere the insufficient body of police arrived at the scene of disturbance. The civic force of the town is totally inadequate to maintain the peace, and to defend property from the attacks of lawless depredators; and *a more efficient, and more numerous corps ought to be immediately organised,* to give power to the law, so often mocked by the daring front of sedition, and outraged by the frantic violence of an ignorant and deluded rabble. The police form, in fact, so weak a screen against the power of the mob, that popular violence is now, in almost every instance, controlled by the presence of a military force.

The wages obtained by operatives in the various branches of the cotton manufacture are, in general, such, as with the exercise of that economy without which wealth itself is wasted, would be sufficient to provide them with all the decent comforts of life—the average wages of all persons employed in the mills (young and old) being from nine to twelve shillings per week. Their means are too often consumed by vice and *improvidence*. But the wages of certain classes are exceedingly meagre. The introduction of the power-loom, though ultimately destined to be productive of the greatest general benefits, has, in the present restricted state of commerce, occasioned some temporary embarrassment, by diminishing the demand for certain kinds of labour, and, consequently, their price. The hand-loom weavers, *existing in this state of transition,* still continue a very extensive class, and though they labour fourteen hours and upwards daily, earn only from five to seven or eight shillings per week. They consist chiefly of Irish, and are affected by all the causes of moral and physical depression which we have enumerated. Ill fed—ill clothed—half sheltered and ignorant;—weaving in close damp cellars, or crowded workshops, it only remains that they should become, as is too frequently the case, demoralised and reckless, to render perfect the portraiture of savage life. Amongst men so situated, the moral check has no influence in preventing the rapid increase of the population. The existence of cheap and redundant labour in the market has, also, a *constant* tendency to lessen its general price, and hence the wages of the English operatives have been exceedingly reduced by this immigration of Irish—their comforts consequently diminished—their manners debased—and the natural influence of manufactures on the people thwarted. We are well convinced that without the numerical and moral influence of this class, on the means and on the character of the people who have had to enter into competition with them in the market of labour, we should have had less occasion to regret the physical and moral degradation of the operative population.

The poor-laws, as at present administered, retain all the evils of the gross and indiscriminate bounty of ancient monasteries. They also fail in exciting the gratitude of the people, and they extinguish the charity of the rich. The custom is not now demanded as the prop of any superstition; nor is it fit that institutions, well calculated to assuage the miseries which feudalism inflicted on its unemployed and unhappy serfs, should be allowed to perpetuate indigence, improvidence, idleness and vice, in a commercial community. The artificial structure of society, in providing security against existing evils, has too frequently neglected the remote moral influence of its arrangements on the community. Humanity rejoices in the consciousness that the poorest may obtain the advantages of skilful care in disease, and that there are asylums for infirmity, age, and decrepitude; but the unlimited extension of benefits, devised by a wise intelligence for the relief of evils which no human prescience could elude, has a direct tendency to encourage amongst the poor apathy concerning present exigencies, and the neglect of a provision for the contingencies of the future.

A rate levied on property for the support of indigence is, in a great degree, a tax on the capital, from whose employment are derived the incentives of industry and the rewards of the frugal, ingenious, and virtuous poor.

If the only test of the application of this fund be *indigence*, without reference to *desert*—be *want*, irrespective of *character*—motives to frugality, self-control and industry are at once removed, and the strong barrier which nature had itself erected to prevent the moral lapse of the entire population is wantonly destroyed. The tax acts as a new burden on the *industrious* poor, already suffering from an enormous pressure, and not only drags within the limits of pauperism unwilling victims, but paralyses with despair the efforts of those whose exertions might otherwise have prolonged their struggle with adversity. The wages of the worthy are often given to encourage the sluggard, the drunkard, and the man whose imprudence entails on the community the precocious burden of his meagre and neglected offspring.

The feeble obstacle raised in the *country* to the propagation of a pauper population by making the indigent chargeable on the estates of the land-owners, is even there rendered almost entirely inefficacious by the too frequent non-residence of the gentry, or the indifference with which this apparently inevitable evil is regarded. In the South of England the fatal error has been committed of paying a certain portion of the wages of able-bodied labourers out of the fund obtained by the poor-rates; and a population is thus created, bound like slaves to toil, and having also like them a right to be maintained. But, in the large towns, the feeble check to the increase of pauperism, which thus exists in some rural districts, is entirely removed. The land is let to speculators who build cottages, the rents of which are collected weekly, a commutation for the rates being often paid by the landlord when they are demanded, which seldom occurs in the lowest description of houses. A married man having thus by law an unquestioned right to a maintenance proportioned to the number of his family, direct encouragement is afforded to improvident marriages. The most destitute and immoral marry to increase their claim on the stipend appointed for them by law, which thus acts as a bounty on the increase of a squalid and debilitated race, who inherit from their parents disease, sometimes deformity, often vice, and always beggary.

The number of labourers thus created diminishes the already scanty wages of that portion of the population still content to endeavour by precarious toil to maintain their honest independence. Desperate is the struggle by which, under such a system, the upright labourer procures for his family the comforts of existence. Many are dragged by the accidents of life to an unwilling acceptance of this legalised pension of the profligate, and some, over informed by misfortune in the treachery of their own hearts, are seduced to palter with temptation, and at length to capitulate with their apparent fate.

Fearful demoralisation attends an impost whose distribution diminishes the incentives to prudence and virtue. When reckless of the future, the intelligence of man is confined to the narrow limits of the present. He thus debases himself beneath the animals, whose instincts teach them to lay up stores for the season of need. The gains of the pauper are, in prosperity, frequently squandered in taverns, whilst his family exists in hungered and ragged misery, and few sympathies with the sufferings of his aged relatives or neighbours enter his cold heart, since he knows they have an equal claim with himself, on that pittance which the law awards. The superfluities which nature would prompt him in a season of abundance to hoard for the accidents of the future, are wasted with reckless profusion; because *the law takes care of the future.* Selfish profligacy usurps the seat of the household virtues of the English labourer.

Charity once extended an invisible chain of sympathy between the higher and lower ranks of society, which has been destroyed by the luckless pseudophilanthropy of the law. Few aged or decrepid pensioners now gratefully receive the visits of the higher classes—few of the poor seek the counsel, the admonitions, and assistance of the rich in the period of the inevitable accidents of life. The bar of the overseer is however crowded with the sturdy applicants for a legalised relief, who regard the distrib-utor of this bounty as their stern and merciless oppressor, instructed by the compassionless rich to reduce to the lowest possible amount the alms which the law wrings from their reluctant hands. This disruption of the natural ties has created a wide gulf between the higher and lower orders of the community, across which the scowl of hatred banishes the smile of charity and love.

That government have appointed a Commission of in-quiry into the evils arising from the administration of the Poor-laws, must be a source of satisfaction to every well-wisher to the poor. Since it would be unjust to annul the existing provision for a rapidly increasing indigence which the law has itself fostered, the improvement of its present administration is all that the most sanguine can expect as an immediate result of this inquiry. Every change which assimilates the *method of distributing* this legal charity to that by which a well-regulated private bounty is administered, must be hailed. The present official organisation in the large towns is incapable of pro-ducing these results. The parish officers and sidesmen are not sufficiently numerous to enable them (if they were permitted by law) to make a discrimination—concerning the characters of individuals, their actual condition, and the accidents or faults that may have occasioned it—equal to that which is observed in the most judicious distribution of private bounty. Since desert does not enhance the claim which indigence can enforce, the only relation which the parish officer now has with the applicant for relief is that of the investigation and proof of his indigence; and, to this end, those now employed may be sufficiently proper agents. But if we would substitute any portion of that sympathy with the distresses of the poor, and that gratitude for relief afforded—that acknowledged right to administer good counsel, and that willingness to receive advice—that privilege of inquiring into the arangements of domestic economy, instructing the ignorant, and checking the perverse—all which attend the beneficent path of private charity, much superior men must be employed in the office of visiting the houses of the poor, and being the almoners of the public. Such an office can only be properly filled by men of some education, but especially of high moral character, and possessing great natural gentleness. An attempt should be constantly made to relieve the mind of the independent poor from the necessity of receiving an eleemosynary dole, by recommending the worthy to employment. It is not sufficient that the Sidesman or Churchwarden should give a few hours daily to an examination of all applicants in our enormous townships, but the towns should be minutely subdivided, each district having its local board, which (besides an executive parish overseer resident in the district, and thus possessing every means of becoming minutely acquainted with the character of the inhabitants), should also be furnished with its board of superior officers. By such means: by adopting the test of desert, at least to determine the *amount* of relief bestowed: by discouraging

or even rejecting those whose indigence is the consequenc
of dissipation, of idleness, and of wilful imprudence; an
by making the overseers themselves the means of instruct
ing the poor, that every labourer is the surest architect o
his own fortune—by constituting them the patrons o
virtue and the censors of vice, and besides being th
almoners of the public charity, the sources of a powerfu
moral agency—much good might be effected. The enoi
mous expenditure, incurred by the present system, migh
be exceedingly reduced, and the alms might at length (b
a process whose success would depend on the gradua
moral improvement of society), be confined to such o
the aged, the decrepid, and the unfortunate, as bein
without the hope of assistance from the charity of rela
tions or friends, were thus reluctantly driven, by a har
necessity, to have recourse to the *fund of the poor. Socie
ties for mutual relief should be everywhere encouraged
and a constant effort should be vigorously maintained t
disburden the public of this enormous tax, by every othe
means which would contribute to the virtuous independ
ence of the working classes.* . . .

The sources of vice and physical degradation are allie
with the causes of pauperism. Amongst the poor, the mos
destitute are too frequently the most demoralised—virtu
is the surest economy—vice is haunted by profligacy an
want. Where there are the most paupers, the gin shops
taverns, and beer houses are most numerous. . . .

There is . . . a licentiousness capable of corruptin
the whole body of society, like an insidious disease, whicl
eludes observation, yet is equally fatal in its effects. Crimi
nal acts may be statistically classed—the victims of th
law may be enumerated—but the number of those affecte
with the moral leprosy of vice cannot be exhibited witl

mathematical precision. Sensuality has no record,[2] and the relaxation of social obligations may coexist with a half dormant, half restless impulse to rebel against all the preservative principles of society; yet these chaotic elements may long smoulder, accompanied only by partial eruptions of turbulence or crime. . . .

One other characteristic of the social body, in its present constitution, appears to us too remarkable and important to be entirely overlooked.

Religion is the most distinguished and ennobling feature of civil communities. Natural attributes of the human mind appear to ensure the culture of some form of worship; and as society rises through its successive stages, these forms are progressively developed, from the grossest observances of superstition, until the truths and dictates of revelation assert their rightful supremacy.

The absence of religious feeling, the neglect of all religious ordinances, afford substantive evidence of so great a moral degradation of the community, as to ensure a concomitant civic debasement. The social body cannot be constructed like a machine, on abstract principles which merely include physical motions, and their numerical results in the production of wealth. The mutual relation of men is not merely dynamical, nor can the composition of their forces be subjected to a purely mathematical calculation. Political economy, though its object be to ascertain the means of increasing the wealth of nations, cannot accomplish its design, without at the same time regarding their happiness, and as its largest ingredient the cultivation of religion and morality.

[2] No record exists by which the number of illegitimate births can be ascertained. Even this evidence would form a very imperfect rule by which to judge of the comparative prevalence of sensuality.

With unfeigned regret, we are therefore constrained to add, that the standard of morality is exceedingly debased, and that religious observances are neglected amongst the operative population of Manchester. The bonds of domestic sympathy are too generally relaxed; and as a consequence, the filial and paternal duties are uncultivated. The artisan has not time to cherish these feelings, by the familiar and grateful arts which are their constant food, and without which nourishment they perish. An apathy benumbs his spirit. Too frequently the father, enjoying perfect health and with ample opportunities of employment, is supported in idleness on the earnings of his oppressed children; and on the other hand, when age and decrepitude cripple the energies of the parents, their adult children abandon them to the scanty maintenance derived from parochial relief.

That religious observances are exceedingly neglected, we have had constant opportunities of ascertaining, in the performance of our duty as Physician to the Ardwick and Ancoats Dispensary, which frequently conducted us to the houses of the poor on Sunday. With rare exceptions, the adults of the vast population of 84,147 contained in Districts Nos. 1, 2, 3, 4, spend Sunday either in supine sloth, in sensuality, or in listless inactivity. A certain portion only of the labouring classes enjoys even healthful recreation on that day, and a very small number frequent the places of worship.

The fruits of external prosperity may speedily be blighted by the absence of internal virtue. With pure religion and undefiled, flourish frugality, forethought, and industry—the social charities which are the links of kindred, neighbours, and societies—and the amenities of life, which banish the jealous suspicion with which one order regards another. In vain may the intellect of man be tortured to devise expedients by which the supply of the necessaries of life may undergo an increase, equivalent to that of population, if the moral check be overthrown. Crime, diseases, pestilence, intestine discord, famine, or foreign war—those agencies which repress the rank overgrowth of a meagre and reckless race—will, by a natural law, desolate a people devoid of prudence and principle, whose numbers constantly press on the limits of the means of subsistence. We therefore regard with alarm the state of those vast masses of our operative population which are acted upon by all other incentives, rather than those of virtue; and are visited by the emissaries of every faction, rather than by the ministers of an ennobling faith.

The present means or methods of religious instruction are, in the circumstances in which our large towns are placed, most evidently inadequate to their end. The labours of some few devoted men—of whom the world is not worthy—in the houses of the poor, are utterly insufficient to produce a deep and permanent moral impression on the people. Some of our laws, as now administered, encourage indigence and vice, and hence arises an increased necessity for the daily exertions of the teachers of religion, to stem that flood of prevailing immorality which threatens to overthrow the best means that political sagacity can devise for the elevation of the people.

The exertions of Dr. Tuckerman, of Boston, in establishing 'a ministry for the poor' have been, until very recently, rather the theme of general and deserved praise, than productive of laudable imitation. This ministration is effected, chiefly by a visitation of the houses of the poor, and he proposes as its objects, religious instruction, uninfluenced by sectarian spirit or opinions:—the relief of the most pressing necessities of the poor—first by a well-regulated charity, and secondarily, by instruction in domestic economy—exhortations to industry—admonition concerning the consequences of vice, and by obtaining work for the deserving and unemployed. The minister should also encourage the education of the children, should prove the friend of the poor in periods of perplexity, and, when the labourer is subdued by sickness, should breathe into his ear the maxims of virtue, and the truths of religion. He might also act as a medium of communication and a link of sympathy, between the higher and lower classes of society. He might become the almoner of the rich, and thus daily sow the seeds of a kindlier relationship than that which now subsists between the wealthy and the destitute. He might also serve as a faithful reporter of the secret miseries which are suffered in the abodes of poverty, unobserved by those to whom he may come to advocate the cause of the abandoned. The prevalence of the principles and the practice of the precepts of Christianity, we may hope, will thus ultimately be made to bind together the now incoherent elements of society.

The success of Dr. Tuckerman's labours in Boston had, before the commencement of a similar plan in Manchester, given rise to several societies for the Christian instruction of the people in the Metropolis, and in other parts of the kingdom. Six such societies are now in operation in Manchester and its out-townships—five amongst the Independent, and one amongst the Unitarian Dissenters. . . . But we regret to add that their number is utterly insufficient to affect the habits of more than a small portion of the population. The vast portions of the town included in the Ancoats, Newtown, and Portland districts, are utterly unoccupied by this beneficent system; and, when it is further observed, that in those districts reside the most indigent and immoral of our poor, it will be at once apparent what need there is of the immediate extension of the same powerful agency to them. . . .

Visiting Manchester, the Metropolis of the commercial system, a stranger regards with wonder the ingenuity and comprehensive capacity, which, in the short space of half a century, have here established the staple manufacture of this kingdom. He beholds with astonishment the establishments of its merchants—monuments of fertile genius and successful design:—the masses of capital which have been accumulated by those who crowd upon its mart, and the restless but sagacious spirit which has made every part of the known world the scene of their enterprise. The sudden creation of the mighty system of commercial organisation which covers this county, and stretches its arms to the most distant seas, attests the power and the dignity of man. Commerce, it appears to such a spectator, here gathers in her storehouses the productions of every clime, that she may minister to the happiness of a favoured race.

When he turns from the great capitalists, he contemplates the fearful strength only of that multitude of the labouring population, which lies like a slumbering giant at their feet. He has heard of the turbulent riots of the people—of machine breaking—of the secret and sullen organisation which has suddenly lit the torch of incendiarism, or well nigh uplifted the arm of rebellion in the land. He remembers that political desperadoes have ever loved to tempt this population to the hazards of the swindling game of revolution, and have scarcely failed. In the midst of so much opulence, however, he has disbelieved the cry of need.

Believing that the natural tendency of unrestricted commerce (unchecked by the prevailing want of educa-

tion, and the incentives afforded by imperfect laws to improvidence and vice), is to develop the energies of society,
to increase the comforts and luxuries of life, and to *elevate
the physical condition* of every member of the social body,
we have exposed, with a faithful, though a friendly hand,
the condition of the lower orders connected with the
manufactures of this town, because we conceive that the
evils affecting them result *from foreign and accidental
causes.* A system, which promotes the advance of civilisation, and diffuses it over the world—which promises to
maintain the peace of nations, by establishing a permanent
international law, founded on the benefits of commercial
association, cannot be inconsistent with the happiness of
the *great mass of the people.* There are men who believe
that the labouring classes are condemned for ever, by an
inexorable fate, to the unmitigated curse of toil, scarcely
rewarded by the bare necessaries of existence, and often
visited by the horrors of hunger and disease—that the
heritage of ignorance, labour, and misery, is entailed upon
them as an eternal doom. Such an opinion might appear
to receive a gloomy confirmation, were we content with
the evidence of fact, derived only from the history of uncivilised races, and of feudal institutions. No modern
Rousseau now rhapsodises on the happiness of the state
of nature. Moral and physical degradation are inseparable
from barbarism. The unsheltered, naked savage, starving
on food common to the denizens of the wilderness, never
knew the comforts contained in the most wretched cabin
of our poor.

Civilisation, to which feudality is inimical, but which
is most powerfully promoted by commerce, surrounds
man with innumerable inventions. It has thus a constant
tendency to multiply, without limit, the comforts of existence, and that by an amount of labour, at all times under-

going an indefinite diminution. It continually expands
the sphere of his relations, from a dependence on his own
limited resources, until it has combined into one mighty
league, alike the members of communities, and the powers
of the most distant regions. The cultivation of the faculties, the extension of knowledge, the improvement of the
arts, enable man to extend his dominion over matter, and
to minister, not merely to all the exigencies, but to the
capricious tastes and the imaginary appetites of his nature.
When, therefore, every zone has contributed its most
precious stores—science has revealed her secret laws—
genius has applied the mightiest powers of nature to familiar use, making matter the patient and silent slave of
the will of man—if want prey upon the heart of the
people, we may strongly presume that, besides the effects
of existing manners, some accidental barrier exists, arresting their natural and rightful supply.

The evils affecting the working classes, *so far from being
the necessary results of the commercial system, furnish
evidence of a disease which impairs its energies, if it does
not threaten its vitality.*

The increase of the manufacturing establishments, and
the consequent colonisation of the district, have been
exceedingly more rapid than the growth of its civic institutions. The eager antagonisation of commercial enterprise has absorbed the attention, and concentrated the
energies, of every member of the community. In this strife
the remote influence of arrangements has sometimes been
neglected, not from the want of humanity, but from the
pressure of occupation, and the deficiency of time. Thus,
some years ago, the internal arrangements of mills (now
so much improved) as regarded temperature, ventilation,
cleanliness, and the proper separation of the sexes, &c.,
were such as to be extremely objectionable. The same

cause has, we think, chiefly occasioned the want of police regulations, to prevent the gross neglect of the streets and houses of the poor.

The great and sudden fluctuations to which trade is liable, are often the sources of severe embarrassment. Sometimes the demand for labour diminishes, and its price consequently falls in a corresponding ratio. On the other hand, the existing population has often been totally inadequate to the required production; and capitalists have eagerly invited a supply of labour from distant counties and the sister kingdom. The colonisation of the Irish was thus first encouraged; and has proved one chief source of the demoralisation, and consequent physical depression of the people.

The effects of this immigration, even when regarded as a simple economical question, do not merely include an equation of the comparative cheapness of labour; its influence on civilisation and morals, as *they tend to affect the production of wealth,* cannot be neglected.

In proof of this, it may suffice to present a picture of the natural progress of barbarous habits. Want of cleanliness, of forethought and economy, are found in almost invariable alliance with dissipation, reckless habits, and disease. The population gradually becomes physically less efficient as the producers of wealth—morally so from idleness—politically *worthless* as having few desires to satisfy, and *noxious* as dissipators of capital accumulated. Were such manners to prevail, the horrors of pauperism would accumulate. A debilitated race would be rapidly multiplied. Morality would afford no check to the increase of the population: crime and disease would be its only obstacles—the licentiousness which indulges its capricious appetite, till it exhausts its power—and the disease which, at the same moment, punishes crime, and sweeps away a hecatomb of its victims. A dense mass, impotent alike of great moral or physical efforts, would accumulate; children would be born to parents incapable of obtaining the necessaries of life, who would thus acquire, through the mistaken humanity of the law, a new claim for support from the property of the public. They would drag on an unhappy existence, vibrating between the pangs of hunger and the delirium of dissipation—alternately exhausted by severe and oppressive toil, or enervated by supine sloth. Destitution would now prey on their strength, and then the short madness of debauchery would consummate its ruin. Crime, which banishes or destroys its victims, and disease and death, are severe but brief natural remedies, which prevent the unlimited accumulation of the horrors of pauperism. Even war and pestilence, when regarded as affecting a population thus demoralised, and politically and physically debased, seem like storms which sweep from the atmosphere the noxious vapours whose stagnation threatens man with death.

Morality is therefore worthy of the attention of the economist, even when considered as simply ministering to the production of wealth. Civilisation creates artificial wants, introduces economy, and cultivates the moral and physical capabilities of society. Hence the introduction of an uncivilised race does not tend even primarily to increase the power of producing wealth, in a ratio by any means commensurate with the cheapness of its labour, and may ultimately retard the increase of the fund for the maintenance of that labour. Such a race is useful only as a mass of animal organisation, which consumes the smallest amount of wages. The low price of the labour of such people depends, however, on the paucity of their wants, and their savage habits. When they assist the production of wealth, therefore, their barbarous habits and consequent moral depression must form a part of the equation. They are only necessary to a state of commerce *inconsistent* with such a reward for labour as is calculated to maintain the standard of civilisation. A few years pass, and they become burdens to a community whose morals and physical power they have depressed; and dissipate wealth which they did not accumulate. . . .

Were an unlimited exchange permitted to commerce, the hours of labour might be reduced, and time afforded for the education and religious and moral instruction of the people. With a virtuous population, engaged in free trade, the existence of redundant labour would be an evil of brief duration, rarely experienced. The unpopular, but alas, too necessary proposals of emigration would no longer be agitated. Ingenuity and industry would draw from the whole world a tribute more than adequate to supply the ever-increasing demands of a civilised nation. . . .

Under these circumstances, every part of the system appears necessary to the preservation of the whole. The profits of trade will not allow a greater remuneration for labour, and competition even threatens to reduce its price. *Whatever time is subtracted from the hours of labour must be accompanied with an equivalent deduction from its rewards;* the restrictions of trade prevent other improvements, and we fear that the condition of the working classes cannot be much improved, until the burdens and restrictions of the commercial system are abolished.

We will yield to none in an earnest and unqualified opposition to the present restrictions and burdens of commerce, and chiefly because they lessen the wages of the lower classes, increase the price of food, and prevent the reduction of the hours of labour:—because they will retard the application of a general and efficient system of education, and thus not merely depress the health, but debase the morals of the poor. Those politicians who propose a serious reduction of the hours of labour, unpreceded by the relief of commercial burdens, seem not to believe that this measure would inevitably depress the wages of the poor, whilst the price of the necessaries of life would continue the same. They appear, also, not to have sufficiently reflected that, if this measure *were unaccompanied by a general system of education,* the time thus bestowed would be wasted or misused. If this depression of wages, coincident with an increase of the time generally spent by an uneducated people in sloth or dissipation, be carefully reflected upon, the advocates of this measure will, perhaps, be less disposed to regard it as one calculated to confer unqualified benefits on the labouring classes. To retrace the upward path from evil and misery is difficult. Health is only acquired after disease, by passing through slow and painful stages. Neither can the evils which affect the operative population be instantly relieved by the exhibition of any single notable remedy.

Men are, it must be confessed, too apt to regard with suspicion those who differ from them in opinion, and rancorous animosity is thus engendered between those whose motives are pure, and between whose opinions only shades of difference exist. We believe that no objection to a reduction of the hours of labour would exist amongst the enlightened capitalists of the cotton trade, if the difficulty of maintaining, under the present restrictions, the commercial position of the country did not forbid it. Were these restrictions abolished, they would cease to fear the competition of their foreign rivals, and the working classes of the community would find them to be the warmest advocates of every measure which could conduce to the physical comfort, or moral elevation of the poor.

A general and efficient system of education would be devised—a more intimate and cordial association would be cultivated between the capitalist and those in his employ—the poor would be instructed in habits of forethought and economy; and, in combination with these great and general efforts to ameliorate their condition, when the restrictions of commerce had been abolished, a reduction in the hours of labour would tend to elevate the moral and physical condition of the people.

We are desirous of adding a few observations on each of these measures. Ere the moral and physical condition of the operative population can be much elevated, a system of national education so extensive and liberal as to supply the wants of the whole labouring population must be introduced. Ignorance is twice a curse—first from its necessarily debasing effects, and then because rendering its victim insensible to his own fate, he endures it with supine apathy. The ignorant are, therefore, properly, the care of the state. Our present means of instruction are confined to Sunday Schools, and a few Lancasterian and National Schools, quite inadequate to the wants of the population. The absence of education is like that of cultivation, the mind untutored becomes a waste, in which prejudices and traditional errors grow as rankly as weeds. In this sphere of labour, as in every other, prudent and diligent culture is necessary to obtain genial products from the soil; noxious agencies are abroad, and, while we refuse to sow the germs of truth and virtue, the winds of heaven bring the winged seeds of error and vice. Moreover, as education is delayed, a stubborn barrenness affects the faculties—want of exercise renders them inapt—he that has never been judiciously instructed, has not only to master the first elements of truth, and to unlearn error, but in proportion as the period has been delayed, will be the difficulty of these processes. What wonder then that the teachers of truth should make little impression on an unlettered population, and that the working classes should become the prey of those *who flatter their passions, adopt their prejudices, or even descend to imitate their manners.*

If a period ever existed when public peace was secured by refusing knowledge to the population, that epoch has lapsed. The policy of governments may have been little able to bear the scrutiny of the people. This may be the reason why the fountains of English literature have been sealed—and the works of our reformers, our patriots, and our confessors—the exhaustless sources of all that is pure and holy, and of good report amongst us—*have not been made accessible and familiar to the poor.* Yet literature of this order is destined to determine the structure of our social constitution, and to become the mould of our national character; and they who would dam up the flood of truth from the lower ground, cannot prevent its silent transudation. A little knowledge is thus inevitable, and it is proverbially a dangerous thing. Alarming disturbances of social order generally commence with *a people only partially instructed.* The preservation of *internal peace,* not less than the improvement of our national institutions, depends on the education of the working classes.

Government, unsupported by popular opinion, is deprived of its true strength, and can only retain its power by the hateful expedients of despotism. Laws which obtain not general consent are dead letters, or obedience to them must be purchased by blood. But ignorance perpetuates the prejudices and errors which contend with the just exercise of a legitimate authority, and makes the people the victims of those ill-founded panics which convulse society, or seduces them to those tumults which disgrace the movements of a deluded populace. Unacquainted with the real sources of their own distress, misled by the artful misrepresentations of men whose element is disorder, and whose food faction can alone supply, the people have too frequently neglected the constitutional expedients by which redress ought only to have been sought, and have brought obloquy on their just cause, by the blind ferocity of those insurrectionary movements, in which they have assaulted the institutions of society. That good government may be stable, the people must be so instructed that they may love that *which they know to be right*.

The present age is peculiarly calculated to illustrate the truth of these observations. When we have equally to struggle against the besotted idolatry of ancient modes, which would retain error, and the headlong spirit of innovation, which, under the pretence of reforming, would destroy—now, hurried wildly onwards to the rocks on which we may be crushed; and then sucked back into the deep,—between this Scylla and that Charybdis, shall we hesitate to guide the vessel of the state, by the power of an enlightened popular opinion! The increase of intelligence and virtue amongst the mass of the people will prove our surest safeguard, in the absence of which, the possessions of the higher orders might be, to an ignorant and brutal populace, like the fair plains of Italy to the destroying Vandal. The wealth and splendour, the refinement and luxury of the superior classes, might provoke the wild inroads of a marauding force, before whose desolating invasion every institution which science has erected, or humanity devised, might fall, and beneath whose feet all the arts and ornaments of civilised life might be trampled. . . .

The education afforded to the poor must be substantial. The mere elementary rudiments of knowledge are chiefly useful, as a means to an end. The poor man will not be made a much better member of society, by being only taught to read and write. His education should comprise such branches of general knowledge as would prove sources of rational amusement, and would thus elevate his tastes above a companionship in licentious pleasures. Those portions of the exact sciences which are connected with his occupation, should be familiarly explained to him, by popular lectures, and *cheap treatises*. To this end, Mechanics' Institutions (partly conducted by the artisans themselves, in order that the interest they feel in them may be constantly excited and maintained) should be multiplied by the patrons of education, among the poor. The ascertained truths of political science should be early taught to the labouring classes, and *correct* political information should be constantly and industriously disseminated amongst them. Were the taxes on periodical publications removed, men of great intelligence and virtue might be induced to conduct journals, established for the express purpose of directing to legitimate objects that restless activity by which the people are of late agitated. Such works, sanctioned by the names of men distinguished for their sagacity, spirit, and integrity, would command the attention and respect of the working classes. The poor might thus be also made to understand their political position in society, and the duties that belong to it—'that [3] they are in a great measure the architects of their own fortune; that what others can do for them is trifling indeed, compared with what they can do for themselves; that they are infinitely more interested in the preservation

[3] J. R. McCulloch, "On the Rise, Progress, Present State and Prospects of the British Cotton Manufacture," *Edinburgh Review,* XLVI (1827).

of public tranquillity than any other class of society; that mechanical inventions and discoveries are always supremely advantageous to them; and that their real interests can only be effectually promoted, by displaying greater prudence and forethought.' They should be instructed in the nature of their domestic and social relations. The evils which imprudent marriages entail on those who contract them, on their unhappy offspring, and on society at large, should be exhibited in the strongest light. The consequence of idleness, improvidence, and moral deviations, should be made the subjects of daily admonition; so that a young man might enter the world, not, as at present, without chart or compass, blown hither and thither by every gust of passion, but, with a knowledge of the dangers to which he is exposed, and of the way to escape them.

The relation between the capitalist and those in his employ, might prove a fruitful source of the most beneficial comments. The misery which the working classes have brought upon themselves, by their mistaken notions on this subject, is incalculable, not to mention the injury which has accrued to capitalists, and to the trade of this country.

Much good would result from a more general and cordial association of the higher and lower orders. In Liverpool a charitable society exists denominated the 'Provident,' whose members include a great number of the most influential inhabitants. The town is subdivided into numerous districts, the inspection and care of each of which is committed to one or two members of the association. They visit the people in their houses—sympathise with their distresses, and minister to the wants of the necessitous; but above all, they acquire by their charity, the right of inquiring into their arrangements—

of instructing them in domestic economy—of recommending sobriety, cleanliness, forethought, and method.

Every capitalist might contribute much to the happiness of those in his employ, by a similar exercise of enlightened charity. He might establish provident associations and libraries amongst his people. Cleanliness, and a proper attention to clothing and diet might be enforced. He has frequent opportunities of discouraging the vicious, and of admonishing the improvident. By visiting the houses of the operatives, he might advise the multiplication of household comforts and the culture of the domestic sympathies. Principle and interest admonish him to receive none into his employ, unless they can produce the most satisfactory attestations to their character.

Above all, he should provide instruction for the children of his workpeople: he should stimulate the appetite for useful knowledge, and supply it with appropriate food.

Happily, the effect of such a system is not left to conjecture. In large towns serious obstacles oppose its introduction; but in Manchester more than one enlightened capitalist confesses its importance, and has made preparations for its adoption. In the country, the facilities are greater; and many establishments might be indicated, which exhibit the results of combined benevolence and intelligence. One example may suffice.

Twelve hundred persons are employed in the factories of Mr. Thomas Ashton, of Hyde. This gentleman has erected commodious dwellings for his workpeople, with each of which he has connected every convenience that can minister to comfort. He resides in their immediate vicinity, and has frequent opportunities of maintaining a cordial association with his operatives. Their houses are well furnished, clean, and their tenants exhibit every indication of health and happiness. Mr. Ashton has also built a school, where 640 children, chiefly belonging to his establishment, are instructed on Sunday, in reading, writing, arithmetic, &c. A library, connected with this school, is eagerly resorted to, and the people frequently read after the hours of labour have expired. An infant school is, during the week, attended by 280 children, and in the evenings others are instructed by masters selected for the purpose. The factories themselves are certainly excellent examples of the cleanliness and order which may be attained, by a systematic and persevering attention to the habits of the artisans. . . .

Capitalists, whose establishments are situated in the country, enjoy many opportunities of controlling the habits and ministering to the comforts of those in their employ, which cannot exist in a large manufacturing town. In the former, the land in the vicinity is generally the property of the manufacturer, and upon this he may build commodious houses, and surround the operative with all the conveniences and attractions of a home. In the town, the land is often in the possession of non-resident proprietors, anxious only to obtain the largest amount of chief rent. It is therefore let in separate lots to avaricious speculators, who (unrestrained by any general enactment, or special police regulation) build without plan, wretched abodes in confused groups, intersected by narrow, unpaved or undrained streets and courts. By this disgraceful system the moral and physical condition of the poor undergoes an inevitable depression. . . .

Private rights ought not to be exercised so as to produce a public injury. The law, which describes and punishes offences against the person and property of the subject, should extend its authority by establishing a social code, in which the rights of communities should be protected from the assaults of partial interests. By exercising its functions in the former case, it does not wantonly interfere with the liberty of the subject, nor in the latter, would it violate the reverence due to the sacred security of property.

The powers obtained by the recent changes in the Police Act of Manchester are retrospective, and exclusively refer to the removal of existing evils: their application must also necessarily be slow. We conceive that special police regulations should be framed for the purpose of preventing the recurrence of that gross neglect of decency and violation of order, whose effects we have described. . . .

The associations of workmen, for protecting the price of labour, have too frequently been so directed, as to occasion increased distress to the operatives, embarrassment to the capitalist, and injury to the trade of the country, whereas, were they properly conducted, they might exercise a generally beneficial influence. No combination can permanently raise the wages of labour above the limit defined by the relation existing between population and capital; but partial monopolies, and individual examples of oppression might, by this means, be removed, and occasions exist, when, on the occurrence of a fresh demand, the natural advance of the price of labour might be hastened. So long, however, as these associations needlessly provoke animosity by the slander of private character, by vexatious and useless interference, and by exciting turbulence and alarm, many of their most legitimate purposes cannot be pursued. Distrust will then prevent masters and workmen from framing regulations for their mutual benefit, such as modes of determining the quantity or quality of work produced, and the collection of correct statistical information—or from combining in applications to government for improvements of the laws which affect commerce. Capitalists, fearing combination amongst their workmen, will conceal the true state of the demand, and thus at one period, the operative will be deprived of that reward of his labour, which he would otherwise obtain, and, at another, will receive no warning of the necessary reduction of manufacturing establishments; which change may thus occur at a period, when, having made no provision for it, he may be least able to encounter the privation of his ordinary means of support. The risks attending the outlay of capital, the extension of the sphere of enterprise, and even the execution of contracts are, by the uncertainty thus introduced into circumstances affecting the supply of labour, exceedingly augmented. Larger stocks must be maintained, less confidence will attend commercial transactions, and an increase of price is necessary to cover these expenses and risks. . . .

The efforts of these associations have not unfrequently occasioned the introduction of machinery into branches of labour, whence skill has been driven to undertake the severer and ill-rewarded occupation of ordinary toil. When machinery thus *suddenly* excludes skilled labour, much greater temporary distress is occasioned to the operative, than by the natural and gradual progress of mechanical improvements. By employing the power of these associations, at periods when an advance of wages has been impossible, or to resist a fall which the influence of natural causes rendered inevitable, the workmen have not only prevented the accumulation of the fund for the maintenance of labour, at a period when the advance of population was unchecked, but they have dissipated their own savings, as well as the monies of the union, in useless efforts, and, when pride and passion have combined to prolong the struggle, their furniture and clothes have been sold, and their family reduced to the extremes of misery. The effects of these 'strikes' are frequently shared by unwilling sufferers, first, among those whose labour cannot be conducted independently of the body which has refused to work, and secondly, by those whose personal will is controlled by the threats or the actual violence of the rest. During the 'strike,' habits of idleness or dissipation are not unfrequently contracted—suspicion degenerates into hatred—and a wide gulf is created between the masters and the workmen. The kindlier feelings are extinguished, secret leagues are formed, property is destroyed, such of the operatives as do not join the combination, are daily assaulted, and at length licence mocks the law with the excesses of popular tumult.

It is impossible that the distrust, thus created, should not sometimes occasion the exclusion from the trade, of the entire body of workmen concerned, and the introduction of a new colony of operatives into the district. The labourers thus immigrating are not seldom an uncivilised and foreign race, so that, if ever the slightest tendency to cordial co-operation existed between the capitalist and the operative, that is now dissolved. The obstinacy with which this struggle with the manufacturer has sometimes been conducted has occasioned the removal of establishments to another district, or even to a foreign country, and these contests are always unfavourable to the introduction of fresh capital into the neighbourhood where they occur.

The more deserving and intelligent portions of the labouring class are often controlled by the greater boldness and activity of that portion which has least knowledge and virtue. Thus, we fear, that the power of the Co-operative Unions has been directed to mischievous objects, and the funds, the time, and energies of the operatives, have been wasted on unfeasible projects. Moreover, they who, as they are the weakest, ought to be, and generally are, the firmest advocates of liberty, have been misled into gross violations of the liberty of their fellow workmen. The power of these unions, to create disorder, or to attain improper objects, would be destroyed, if every assault were prosecuted, or the violation of the liberty of the subject prevented by the assiduous interference of an efficient police. The radical remedy for these evils is such an education as shall teach the people in what consists their true happiness, and how their interests may be best promoted.

The tendency to these excesses would be much diminished, did a cordial sympathy unite the higher with the lower classes of society. The intelligence of the former should be the fountain whence this should flow. If the *results* of labour be solely regarded, in the connection of the capitalist with those in his employ, the first step is taken towards treating them as a mere animal power necessary to the mechanical processes of manufacture. This is a heartless, if not a degrading association. The contract for the rewards of labour conducted on these principles issues in suspicion, if not in rancorous animosity.

The operative population constitutes one of the most important elements of society, and when numerically considered, the magnitude of its interests and the extent of its power assume such vast proportions, that the folly which neglects them is allied to madness. If the higher classes are unwilling to diffuse intelligence among the lower, those exist who are ever ready to take advantage of their ignorance; if they will not seek their confidence, others will excite their distrust; if they will not endeavour to promote domestic comfort, virtue, and knowledge among them, their misery, vice, and prejudice will prove volcanic elements, by whose explosive violence the structure of society may be destroyed. The principles developed in this Pamphlet, as they are connected with facts occurring within a limited sphere of observation, may be unwittingly supposed to have relation to that locality alone. The object of the author will, however, be grossly misunderstood, if it be conceived, that he is desirous of placing in invidious prominence defects which he may have observed in the social constitution of his own town. He believes the evils here depicted to be incident, in a much larger degree, to many other great cities, and the means of cure here indicated to be equally capable of application there. His object is simply to offer to the public *an example* of what he conceives to be too generally the state of the working classes, throughout the kingdom, and to illustrate by *specific instances,* evils everywhere requiring the immediate interference of legislative authority.

SOURCE: *Four Periods of Public Education as Reviewed in 1832—1839—1846—1862 in Papers by Sir James Kay-Shuttleworth, Bart.* (London, 1862), pp. 3–5, 7–12, 21–29, 33–34, 37–41, 48–53, 58–66, 69–75. The title appearing above is the one used by Kay-Shuttleworth in 1862. The original title of the pamphlet was *The Moral and Physical Condition of the Working Classes Employed in the Cotton Manufacture in Manchester.*

2

Recent Measures for the Promotion
of Education in England
(1839)

*Kay-Shuttleworth wrote this pamphlet shortly after as-
suming his duties as secretary to the new created Committee of the Privy Council on Education. Published anony-
mously, it was intended as an explanation and justifica-
tion of the government's policies. It embodies the most
forceful expression of Kay-Shuttleworth's conception of
popular education as an instrument of social control.
Appalled by the Chartist demand for manhood suffrage,
he emphasizes the value of education as a barrier against
subversion and radicalism.*

*In his collection Kay-Shuttleworth assigned this pam-
phlet to the second period in the history of public education, when the central government began to show an interest in the problem. "The Second Period," he wrote in
1862, "opens a more agreeable task to the Author."*

All plans which have been proposed for promoting National Education in England by calling into operation
the powers of the Executive Government, have necessarily
been subjected to the most searching scrutiny. The advocates of education must not, however, accept the earnest-

ness with which public attention is directed to this subject as a measure of the degree in which the necessity of
an extension and improvement of the elementary education of the poorer classes is recognised. It is indeed
generally known that even the art of reading has been
acquired by a portion only of the rising population, and
by a smaller part of the adult working class; and that, as
respects the rudimentary knowledge which might develop
the understanding, and afford the labourer a clear view
of his social position,—its duties, its difficulties, and rewards,—and thus enable him better to employ the powers
with which Providence has gifted him, to promote his own
comfort and the well-being of society, he is generally destitute, and, what is worse, abandoned to the ill-regulated
and often pernicious agencies by which he is surrounded.
It is commonly confessed that no sufficient means exist to
train the habits of the children of our poorer classes,—to
inspire them with healthful, social, and household sympathies,—with a love of domestic peace and social order,—
with an enlightened reverence for revealed truth,—and
with the sentiment of piety and devotion.

But while these proofs of the fatal void in our national
institutions are admitted, we fear we may not attribute
the eagerness with which every proposal for the improvement and extension of popular education is discussed
solely to an earnest and enlightened sympathy with the
condition of the working classes. We must admit as a necessary element of our estimate of the popular feeling, the
fact that the connection which exists in every well-devised
plan for National Education between the secular and the
religious instruction and moral training of the people,
rouses the advocates of the antagonist principles involved
in questions of civil and religious liberty, which have
caused political struggles deeply affecting the middle and

higher classes of society, but in the consequences of which the lower classes have hitherto had comparatively little practical interest.

The ferment occasioned by the recent settlement of some of these grave questions has not yet subsided; and to the state of public opinion, which has had its source in their prolonged discussion, we must attribute, in a great degree, the suspicion with which every proposal for the promotion of National Education is regarded, and the singular excitement produced by its announcement.

We are the last to deprecate public discussion—we invite it: we rejoice in the activity of the public mind—we have nothing to fear excepting from its apathy; our hopes are all concentrated in the right of private opinion—in the freedom with which, in this country, every question of public policy is debated, and in the consequent spread of a knowledge of the principles on which the changes demanded by the advance of civilisation are based.

In the first movements of popular excitement, misrepresentation and clamour may mislead individuals or entire political or religious bodies into an opposition to plans, which on more attentive consideration they would have cordially approved. Nay, in any society in which the right of public discussion is admitted, it is the lot of every improvement to be misunderstood and misrepresented at its first announcement; the frame of society receives a shock at every change, even for the better, and in the first moments of surprise the entire community bestirs itself to ascertain whence comes the disturbance, and what is its object.

To enable every person interested in this national question to ascertain what is the plan of her Majesty's Government, and thus to prevent or to remove the consequences of industriously circulated misrepresentations;—to invite public discussion, and at the same time to provide it with a plain exposition of the principles and arrangements which we conceive to be involved in that plan, we have published the Report of the Committee of Council approved by her Majesty, with a few observations. . . .

. . . The rapid progress of our physical civilisation has occasioned the growth of masses of manufacturing population, the instruction, and moral, and religious elevation of which have hitherto been neglected by the State. These communities exhibit alarming features; labouring classes, unmatched in the energy and hardihood with which they pursue their daily toil, yet thriftless, incapable of husbanding their means, or resisting sensual gratification; high wages and want under the same roof; while other portions of the same classes are struggling on the barest pittance with continual labour, abstinent by necessity. From opposite quarters misery and discontent are goading both. . . .

Physical prosperity stimulates all the animal appetites, and, if unaided by moral restraint, wastes her resources, and, instead of connecting content and peace with plenty, continually rouses the population to feverish exertion. Notwithstanding the high wages of the artisan, the wife commits her infant to an hireling, and leaves her domestic duties to work in the manufactory. The parents, to enable ill-regulated means to satisfy increasing wants, lead their children of a tender age to the same scene of continual exertion. Domestic virtue and household piety have little opportunity to thrive in a population alternating between protracted labour and repose, or too frequent sensual gratification. When all the animal powers are thus continually called into action, adversity is met with sullen discontent, or with fierce outbreaks of passionate disquiet.

Whoever will promise less toil and more money, is a prophet in the manufacturing districts; and—in the absence of those who would teach, that comfort can only be secured by a cultivation of those domestic sympathies and household virtues, which spring from a well-regulated mind, and prove that happiness depends upon those internal moral resources, without which the greatest prosperity is often a curse—prophets will always be found ready to teach the population to seek a remedy for the evils they endure by violent attempts at social change. To the ignorant man, who has only the sense or the continual necessity to labour, in order to gratify his unappeased desires for sensual gratification, and to meet the wants created by wasted means, who can be more welcome than he who comes with the golden promise of high wages and ease, instead of leading him to an enlightened estimate of his domestic and social duties, and teaching him how much a resolute will, under the influence of morality and religion, may do, even in adverse circumstances, to render the lot of the poor man peaceful and happy? Less work and more means have always, therefore, been the promises of every impostor who has practised on the ignorance, discontent, and suffering of the manufacturing population.

We shall have to speak, in subsequent pages, of the political and social combinations which have of late prevailed in the manufacturing districts; the Trades' Unions, in which incendiarism, personal violence, and even assassination, are practised for the unattainable object of sustaining the rate of wages above the level resulting from the natural laws of trade—and the more recent armed associations for political purposes, in which the working classes have been exhorted to obtain by force privileges withheld by the constitutional representatives of the people; results, which are all ascribable to the fact that the physical development of the population has been more rapid than the growth of our intellectual, moral, and religious institutions.

On the other hand, it is cheering to know, that the accumulation of the people in masses renders them more accessible to the beneficial influence of well-regulated social institutions. Having once encountered the necessity of supplying the intellectual and moral wants of the labouring classes, knowledge and virtue will, with adequate agencies, make more rapid progress among a concentrated than a scattered population. So long as our artisans lived in cottages scattered over the moors of our northern, and the wolds of our southern counties, little danger might arise to the State from their universal ignorance, apathy, and want; but if the necessity for raising their moral and intellectual condition could, under such circumstances, have been as pressing as it now is, the difficulty of civilising them would have been almost insuperable. In the concentrated population of our towns, the dangers arising from the neglect of the intellectual and moral culture of the working class are already imminent; and the consequences of permitting another generation to rise, without bending the powers of the executive government and of society to the great work of civilisation and religion, for which the political and social events of every hour make a continual demand, must be social disquiet little short of revolution. But the same masses of population are equally open to all the beneficial influences derivable from a careful cultivation of their domestic and social habits; from the communication of knowledge enabling them to perceive their true relation to the other classes of society, and how dependent their interests are upon the stability of our institutions and the preservation of social order.

The law recognises the duty devolving on property, as respects the education of the factory children; and we rejoice to believe that, under the guidance of men of high intelligence and benevolence, such as many of the most wealthy manufacturers are, we shall soon realise what are the fruits of a well-devised system of intellectual, moral, and religious training, in rendering the communities, in whose well-being they have so deep a stake, examples of what may be effected by applying to the moral elevation of the population the same sagacity and perseverance which have occasioned its physical prosperity. A short time only will elapse before, in some of our great towns, the most influential inhabitants will combine for the erection and support of Model Schools. Such institutions will create and diffuse a more correct estimate of the value of Education, and will promote its spread.

For another neglected class also the State has interfered. Under the parochial system, the orphan, deserted, and illegitimate children—waifs of society—were scattered through the parochial workhouses of England, where they were promiscuously mingled with the idiots, the sick, the sturdy vagabond, and profligate women. From the parochial workhouses, the gaols and hulks recruited the ranks of crime. These children are now under the care of Boards of Guardians, separated from the adult paupers, and measures are in progress to educate them so as to render them efficient and virtuous members of society.

For the juvenile offenders the Government is carefully preparing a system of reformatory discipline and training, in which all the resources of the educator will be exhausted to redeem these outcasts from the depravity consequent on neglect and evil example.

Besides these signs of coming improvement, we hail, as a presage of no little importance, the fact that the subject of National Education has occupied the attention of the Houses of Parliament during five nights of anxious discussion. We never were so sanguine as to expect that the great embarrassments with which it is surrounded could be at once dispelled; but we have a confident belief that every hour increases the anxiety of all friends of our constitutional liberties and national institutions, to preserve both by the education of the people. . . .

But if this be the state of primary education in the Continental States, what, we are entitled to ask, ought to be its condition in England? Our political atmosphere has been comparatively serene; our social institutions have not suffered the shock of any disastrous revolution; our country has not been ravaged, as has been the fate of every Continental state, by any armies. The great territorial possessions of our aristocracy, are but so many stores of wealth and power, by which the civilisation of the people might be promoted. In every English proprietor's domain there ought to be, as in many there are, school-houses with well trained masters, competent and zealous to rear the population in obedience to the laws, in submission to their superiors, and to fit them to strengthen the institutions of their country by their domestic virtues, their sobriety, their industry, and forethought,—by the steadiness of purpose with which they pursue their daily labour,—by the enterprise with which they recover from calamity,—and by the strength of heart with which they are prepared to grapple with the enemies of their country. How striking is the contrast which the estates of the landed proprietors of almost all other European countries bear in all that relates to material wealth—to the domains of our English aristocracy! On the Continent you are met on every side by the proofs of meagre or exhausted resources. In England we have no excuse; we have proofs of how much can be affected, and at how little cost, by the well directed energy of individuals; and we have in our eye examples among our peerage which cannot but be imitated as soon as they are generally known and appreciated.

Our great commercial cities and manufacturing towns contain middle classes whose wealth, enterprise, and intelligence have no successful rivals in Europe; they have made this country the mart of the whole earth; they have covered the seas with their ships, exploring every inlet, estuary, or river which affords them a chance of successful trade. They have colonised almost every accessible region; and from all these sources, as well as from the nightly and daily toil of our working classes in mines, in manufactories, and workshops, in every form of hardy and continued exertion on the sea and on the shore, wealth has been derived, which has supported England in unexampled struggles; yet between the merchants and manufacturers of this country and the poorer class there is little or no alliance, excepting that of mutual interest. But the critical events of this very hour are full of warning, that the ignorance—nay the barbarism—of large portions of our fellow-countrymen, can no longer be neglected, if we are not prepared to substitute a military tyranny or anarchy for the moral subjection which has hitherto been the only safeguard of England. At this hour military force alone retains in subjection great masses of the operative population, beneath whose outrages, if not thus restrained, the wealth and institutions of society would fall. The manufacturers and merchants of England must know what interest they have in the civilisation of the working population; and ere this we trust they are conscious, not merely how deep is their stake in the moral, intellectual, and religious advancement of the labouring class, but how deep is their responsibility to employ for this end the vast resources at their command.

In one other respect England stands in the strongest contrast with the Continental States as to the extent of her means for educational improvement. It is scarcely credible that, with primary education in utter ruin, we should possess educational endowments to the extent of half a million annually, which are either, to a large extent, misapplied, or are used for the support of such feeble and inefficient methods of instruction as to render little service to the community. Whenever the Government shall bend its efforts to combine, for the national advantage, all these great resources, we have no fears for our country. We perceive in it energies possessed by no other nation—partly attributable to the genius of our race; to a large extent derived from the spirit of our policy, which has admitted constant progression in our social institutions; in no small degree to our insular situation, which makes the sea at once the guardian of our liberties and the source of our wealth. But any further delay in the adoption of energetic measures for the elementary education of her working classes is fraught both with intestine and foreign danger—no one can stay the physical influences of wealth —some knowledge the people will acquire by the mere intercourse of society—many appetites are stimulated by a mere physical advancement. With increasing wants comes an increase of discontent, among a people who have only knowledge enough to make them eager for additional enjoyments, and have never yet been suffi- ciently educated to frame rational wishes and to pursue them by rational means. The mere physical influences of civilisation will not, we fear, make them more moral or religious, better subjects of the State, or better Christians, unless to these be superadded the benefits of an education calculated to develope the entire moral and intellectual capacity of the whole population.

A great change has taken place in the moral and intellectual state of the working classes during the last half century. Formerly, they considered their poverty and sufferings as inevitable, as far as they thought about their origin at all; now, rightly or wrongly, they attribute their sufferings to political causes; they think that by a change in political institutions their condition can be enormously ameliorated. The great Chartist petition, recently presented by Mr. Attwood, affords ample evidence of the prevalence of the restless desire for organic changes, and for violent political measures, which pervades the manufacturing districts, and which is every day increasing. This agitation is no recent matter; it has assumed various other forms in the last thirty years, in all of which the manufacturing population have shown how readily masses of ignorance, discontent, and suffering may be misled. At no period within our memory have the manufacturing districts been free from some form of agitation for unattainable objects referable to these causes. At one period, Luddism prevailed; at another, machine-breaking; at successive periods the Trades' Unions have endeavoured in strikes, by hired bands of ruffians, and by assassination, to sustain the rate of wages above that determined by the natural laws of trade; panics have been excited among the working classes, and severe runs upon the Savings' Banks effected from time to time. At one time they have been taught to believe that they could obtain the same wages if an eight hours' bill were passed as if the law permitted them to labour twelve hours in the day; and mills were actually worked on this principle for some weeks, to rivet the conviction in the minds of the working class. The agitation becomes constantly more systematic and better organised, because there is a greater demand for it among the masses, and it is more profitable to the leaders. It is vain to hope that this spirit will subside spontaneously, or that it can be suppressed by coercion. Chartism, an armed political monster, has at length sprung from the soil on which the struggle for the forcible repression of these evils has occurred. It is as certain as any thing future is certain, that the anarchical spirit of the Chartist association will, if left to the operation of the causes now in activity, become every year more formidable. The Chartists think that it is in the power of Government to raise the rate of wages by interfering between the employer and the workman; they imagine that this can be accomplished by a maximum of prices and minimum of wages, or some similar contrivance; and a considerable portion of them believe that the burden of taxation and of all 'fixed charges' (to use Mr. Attwood's expression) ought to be reduced by issuing inconvertible paper, and thus depreciating the currency. They are confident that a Parliament chosen by universal suffrage would be so completely under the dominion of the working classes as to carry these measures into effect; and therefore they petition for universal suffrage, treating all truly remedial measures as unworthy of their notice, or as obstacles to the attainment of the only objects really important. Now the sole effectual means of preventing the tremendous evils with which the anarchical spirit of the manufacturing population threatens the country is, by giving the working people a good secular education, to enable them to understand the true causes which determine their physical condition and regulate the distribution of wealth among the several classes of society. Sufficient intelligence and information to appreciate these causes might be diffused by an education which could easily be brought within the reach of the entire population, though it would necessarily comprehend more than the mere mechanical rudiments of knowledge.

We are far from being alarmists; we write neither under the influence of undue fear, nor with a wish to inspire undue fear into others. The opinions which we have expressed are founded on a careful observation of the proceedings and speeches of the Chartists, and of their predecessors in agitation in the manufacturing districts for many years, as reported in their newspapers; and have been as deliberately formed as they are deliberately expressed. We confess that we cannot contemplate with unconcern the vast physical force which is now moved by men so ignorant and so unprincipled as the Chartist leaders; and without expecting such internal convulsions as may deserve the name of *civil war,* we think it highly probable that persons and property will, in certain parts of the country, be so exposed to violence as materially to affect the prosperity of our manufactures and commerce, to shake the mutual confidence of mercantile men, and to diminish the stability of our political and social institutions. That the country will ultimately recover from these internal convulsions we think, judging from its past history, highly probable; but the recovery will be effected by the painful process of teaching the working classes, by actual experience, that the violent measures which they desire do not tend to improve their condition.

It is astonishing to us, that the party calling themselves Conservative should not lead the van in promoting the diffusion of that knowledge among the working classes which tends beyond any thing else to promote the security of property and the maintenance of public order. To restore the working classes to their former state of incurious and contented apathy is impossible, if it were desirable. If they are to have knowledge, surely it is the part of a wise and virtuous Government to do all in its power to secure to them useful knowledge, and to guard them against pernicious opinions.

We have already said that all instruction should be hallowed by the influence of religion; but we hold it to be equally absurd and short-sighted to withhold secular instruction, on the ground that religion is alone sufficient.

We do not, however, advocate that form of religious instruction which merely loads the memory, without developing the understanding, or which fails to stir the sympathies of our nature to their inmost springs. There is a form of instruction in religion which leaves the recipient at the mercy of any religious or political fanatic who may dare to use the sacred pages as texts in support of imposture. We have seen that even a maniac may lead the people to worship him as the Messiah, whose second coming, spoken of in the pages of Holy Writ, was fulfilled. Many of the Chartists proclaim themselves Missionaries of Christianity. They know how to rouse the superstition of an ignorant population in favour of their doctrines, by employing passages of Scripture the true meaning of which the uninstructed mass do not reach. They continually set before them those verses which speak of the rich man as an oppressor—which show with how much difficulty the rich shall enter the kingdom of heaven. Poverty is the Lazarus whom they place in Abraham's bosom— wealth the Dives whom they doom to hell. They find passages in the writings of the Apostles speaking of a community of goods among the early Christians: on this they found the doctrines of the Socialists. Our Saviour, in the

synagogue of Nazareth, opened the Scripture at the proph-
ecy in which Isaiah describes His divine mission: 'The
Spirit of the Lord is upon me, because he hath anointed
me to preach the gospel to the poor, &c.' From these and
similar passages, they gather the sanctions of their own
Mission. Christianity in their hands becomes the most
frantic democracy, and democracy is clothed with the
sanctions of religion. Even the arming of the Chartist
association is derived from our Saviour's injunction, 'he
that hath no sword, let him sell his garment and buy one.'
To such purposes may the Scriptures be wrested by unscrupulous men who have practised on the ignorance,
discontent, and suffering of the mass.

Their power will continue as long as the people are
without sufficient intelligence to discern in what the fearful error of such impiety consists. There are times in
which it is necessary that every man should be prepared
to give a reason for the faith that is in him. We loathe
a merely speculative religion, which does not purify the
motives, and which robs piety alike of humility and charity; but when the teachers of the great mass of the people
unite the imposture of religious and political fanatics,
preaching anti-social doctrines as though they were a
gospel of truth, the knowledge of the people must be
increased, and their intellectual powers strengthened, so
as to enable them to grapple with the error and to overcome it.

Next to the prevalence of true religion, we most ear-
nestly desire that the people should know how their interests are inseparable from those of the other orders of
society; and we will not stop to demonstrate so obvious
a truth as that secular knowledge, easily accessible, but
most powerful in its influence, is necessary to this end.

If, on the other hand, an opponent of popular educa-

tion should admit the existence of the evil and the suf-
ficiency of the remedy, but should refuse to apply it because it would violate his notions of the duty of the Government to diffuse the orthodox faith, we can only say
that such a person is unfit for the government of men in
the nineteenth century, and that he is sacrificing to his
own opinions upon abstruse questions of theology, the
certain and demonstrable temporal happiness of millions
of his fellow-creatures.

SOURCE: *Four Periods*, pp. 187–189, 202–206, 227–234.

3

First Report on the Training School
at Battersea
(1841)

*One of Kay-Shuttleworth's most important achievements
in the Minutes of 1846 was the creation of a system of
teacher recruitment and training. This selection shows
how his ideas on teacher training were shaped by his initial interest in schools for pauper children and by his
assumption that one form of education was required for
"the middle or upper classes of society" and another for
"the poor." On the other hand, it should also be noted—
borrowing the language of twentieth-century American
education—that although Kay-Shuttleworth assumed that
the education of the poor would be "separate" he was
determined that it would not be "unequal." The Report
provides a good example of his zeal in seeking out the best
and most advanced educational methods for the schools
of the poor. His enthusiasm for Pestalozzian principles is
very much in evidence.*

*As an Assistant Poor Law Commissioner stationed in
East Anglia from 1835 to 1838, Kay-Shuttleworth had
taken an active interest in the education of pauper children. After his transfer to the metropolitan area, he
launched a major educational enterprise at Norwood, in*

an institution housing over a thousand pauper children from London. He continued to serve as an Assistant Commissioner for two more years after his appointment to the Education Committee. In August, 1839, he joined E. Carleton Tufnell, another Assistant Poor Law Commissioner, in a trip to the Continent to study normal schools. They were especially impressed with Pestalozzian schools in Switzerland. On their return to England they decided to use their own funds to establish a training school on the Swiss model at Battersea. Kay-Shuttleworth's Report, addressed to the Poor Law Commission, describes that enterprise.

January 1, 1841.

Gentlemen,

The efforts made by your Assistant Commissioners for the improvement of the training of pauper children in the rural and metropolitan districts, made apparent, at a very early period, the great difficulty of procuring the assistance of schoolmasters and schoolmistresses acquainted with the principles on which the education of this class of children ought to be conducted. . . .

The training of pauper children in a workhouse or district School cannot be successful unless the teacher be moved by Christian charity to the work of rearing in religion and industry the outcast and orphan children of our rural and city population. The difficulty of redeeming by education the mischief wrought in generations of a vicious parentage can be estimated only by those who know how degenerate these children are.

The pauper children assembled at Norwood, from the garrets, cellars, and wretched rooms of alleys and courts, in the dense parts of London, are often sent thither in a low state of destitution, covered only with rags and ver-

min; often the victims of chronic disease; almost universally stunted in their growth; and sometimes emaciated
with want. The low-browed and inexpressive physiog-
nomy or malign aspect of the boys is a true index to the
mental darkness, the stubborn tempers, the hopeless spirits, and the vicious habits, on which the master has to
work. He needs no small support from Christian faith and
charity for the successful prosecution of such a labour;
and no quality can compensate for the want of that spirit
of self-sacrifice and tender concern for the well-being of
these children, without which their instruction would be
anything but a labour of love. A baker or a shoemaker,
or a shop apprentice, or commercial clerk, cannot be expected to be imbued with this spirit during a residence
of six months in the neighbourhood of a Model School
if he has not imbibed it previously at its source.

The men who undertake this work should not set about
it in the spirit of hirelings, taking the speediest means to
procure a maintenance with the least amount of trouble.
A commercial country will always offer irresistible temptations to desert such a profession, to those to whom the
annual stipend is the chief, if not sole, motive to exertion.
The outcast must remain neglected, if there be no principle, which, even in the midst of a commercial people, will
enable men to devote themselves to this vocation from
higher motives than the mere love of money.

Experience of the motives by which the class of schoolmasters now plying their trade in this country are commonly actuated, is a graver source of want of confidence
in their ability to engage in this labour than the absence
of skill in their profession. A great number of them undertake these duties either because they are incapacitated by
age or infirmity for any other, or because they have failed
in all other attempts to procure a livelihood; or because,

in the absence of well-qualified competitors the least amount of exertion and talent enables the most indolent schoolmasters to present average claims on public confidence and support. Rare indeed are the examples in which skill and principle are combined in the agents employed in this most important sphere of national self-government. Other men will not enable you to restore the children of vagabonds and criminals to society, purged of the taint of their parents' vices, and prepared to perform their duties as useful citizens in a humble sphere.

The peculiarities of the character and condition of the pauper children demand the use of appropriate means for their improvement. The general principles on which the education of children of all classes should be conducted are doubtless fundamentally the same; but for each class specific modifications are requisite, not only in the methods but in the matter of instruction.

The discipline, management, and methods of instruction in elementary schools for the poor, differ widely from those which ought to characterise Schools for the middle or upper classes of society. The instruction of the blind, of the deaf and dumb, of criminals, of paupers, and of children in towns and in rural districts, renders necessary the use of a variety of distinct methods in order to attain the desired end.

The peculiarity of the pauper child's condition is, that his parents, either from misfortune, or indolence, or vice, have sunk into destitution. In many instances children descend from generations of paupers. They have been born in the worst purlieus of a great city, or in the most wretched hovels on the parish waste. They have suffered privation of every kind. Perhaps they have wandered about the country in beggary, or have been taught the arts of petty thieving in the towns. They have lived with brutal and cruel men and women, and have suffered from their caprice and mismanagement. They have seen much of vice and wretchedness, and have known neither comfort, kindness, nor virtue.

If they are sent very young to the workhouse, their entire training in religious knowledge, and in all the habits of life, devolves on the schoolmaster. If they come under his care at a later period, his task is difficult in proportion to the vicious propensities he has to encounter.

The children to whose improvement Pestalozzi devoted his life were of a similar class,—equally ignorant, and perhaps equally demoralised, in consequence of the internal discords attendant on the revolutionary wars, which at the period when his labours commenced had left Switzerland in ruin.

The class of children which De Fellenberg placed under the charge of Vehrli at Hofwyl were in like manner picked up on the roads of the canton—they were the outcasts of Berne.

These circumstances are among the motives which led us to a careful examination of the Schools of Industry and Normal Schools of the cantons of Switzerland. These schools are more or less under the influence of the lessons which Pestalozzi and De Fellenberg have taught that country. They differ in some important particulars from those which exist in England, and the experience of Switzerland in this peculiar department of elementary instruction appears pre-eminently worthy of attention.

Those Orphan and Normal Schools of Switzerland which have paid the deference due to the lessons of Pestalozzi and De Fellenberg, are remarkable for the gentleness and simplicity of the intercourse between the scholar and his master. The formation of character is always kept in mind as the great aim of education. The intelligence is enlightened, in order that it may inform the conscience, and that the conscience, looking forth through this intelligence, may behold a wider sphere of duty, and have at its command a greater capacity for action. The capacity for action is determined by the cultivation of habits appropriate to the duties of the station which the child must occupy.

Among the labouring class no habit is more essential to virtuous conduct than that of steady and persevering labour. Manual skill connects the intelligence with the brute force with which we are endued. The instruction in elementary Schools should be so conducted, as not only to assist the labourer in acquiring mechanical dexterity, but in bringing his intelligence to aid the labours of his hands, whether by a knowledge of the principles of form or numbers, or of the properties of natural objects, and the nature of the phenomena by which his labours are likely to be affected. In a commercial country it is preeminently important to give him such an acquaintance with geography as may stimulate enterprise at home, or may tend to swell the stream of colonisation which is daily extending the dominion of British commerce and civilisation. Labour, which brings the sweat upon the brows, requires relaxation, and the child should therefore learn to repose from toil among innocent enjoyments, and to avoid those vicious indulgences which waste the labourer's strength, rob his house of comfort, and must sooner or later be the source of sorrow. There is a dignity in the lot of man in every sphere, if it be not cast away. The honour and the joy of successful toil should fill the labourer's songs in his hour of repose. From religion man learns that all the artificial distinctions of society are as nothing before that God who searcheth the heart. Religion therefore raises the labourer to the highest dignity of human existence, the knowledge of the will and the enjoyment of the favour of God. Instructed by religion, the labourer knows how in daily toil he fulfils the duties and satisfies the moral and natural necessities of his existence, while the outward garb of mortality is gradually wearing off, and the spirit preparing for emancipation.

An education guided by the principles described in this brief sketch, appears to us appropriate to the preparation of the outcast and orphan children for the great work of a Christian's life.

After a trial of various expedients, to which allusion has been made in preceding Reports, it became apparent that the means of embracing within one comprehensive plan the training of the 50,000 pauper children now in the workhouses did not exist in this country; and the importance of not abandoning these children to the consequences of the misfortunes and vices of their parents grew in proportion to the difficulties with which the subject was encumbered.

That which seemed most important was the preparation of a class of teachers who would cheerfully devote themselves, and with anxious and tender solicitude, to rear these children, abandoned by all natural sympathies, as a wise and affectionate parent would prepare them for the duties of life.

To so grave a task as an attempt to devise the means of training these teachers, it was necessary to bring a patient and humble spirit, in order that the results of experience in this department might be examined, and that none that were useful might be hastily thrown aside. Our examination of the continental Schools was undertaken with this view. . . .

In the Orphan Schools which have emanated from Pestalozzi and De Fellenberg, we found the type which has assisted us in our subsequent labours. In walking with M. De Fellenberg through Hofwyl, we listened to the precepts which we think most applicable to the education of the pauper class. In the Normal School of the Canton of Thurgovia, and in the Orphan Schools of St. Gall and Appenzell, we found the development of those principles so far successful as to assure us of their practical utility.

The Normal School at Kruitzlingen is in the summer palace of the former abbot of the convent of that name, on the shore of the Lake of Constance, about one mile from the gate of the city. The pupils are sent thither, from the several communes of the canton, to be trained three years by Vehrli, before they take charge of the Communal Schools. . . .

Some of the other Normal Schools of Switzerland are remarkable for the same simplicity in their domestic arrangements, though the students exceed in their intellectual attainments all notions prevalent in England of what should be taught in such schools. Thus in the Normal School of the canton of Berne the pupils worked in the fields during eight hours of the day, and spent the rest in intellectual labour. They were clad in the coarsest dresses of the peasantry, wore wooden shoes, and were without stockings. Their intellectual attainments, however, would have enabled them to put to shame the masters of most of our best elementary schools.

Such men, we felt assured, would go forth cheerfully to their humble village homes to spread the doctrine which Vehrli taught of peace and contentment in virtuous exertion; and men similarly trained appeared to us best fitted for the labour of reclaiming the pauper youth of England to the virtues, and restoring them to the happiness of her best instructed peasantry.

We therefore cherished the hope that on this plan a

Normal School might be founded for the training of the teachers, to whom the schools for pauper children might be usefully committed. The period seemed to be unpropitious for any public proposals on this subject. We were anxious that a work of such importance should be undertaken by the authorities most competent to carry it into execution successfully, and we painfully felt how inadequate our own resources and experience were for the management of such an experiment; but after various inquiries, which were attended with few encouraging results, we thought that as a last resort we should not incur the charge of presumption, if, in private and unaided, we endeavoured to work out the first steps of the establishment of an institution for the training of teachers, which we hoped might afterwards be intrusted to abler hands. We determined therefore to devote a certain portion of our own means to this object, believing that when the scheme of the institution was sufficiently mature to enable us to speak of results rather than of anticipations, the well-being of 50,000 pauper children would plead its own cause with the government and the public, so as to secure the future prosperity of the establishment.

The task proposed was, to reconcile a simplicity of life not remote from the habits of the humbler classes, with such proficiency in intellectual attainments, such a knowledge of method, and such skill in the art of teaching, as would enable the pupils selected to become efficient masters of elementary schools. We hoped to inspire them with a large sympathy for their own class. To implant in their minds the thought that their chief honour would be to aid in rescuing that class from the misery of ignorance and its attendant vices. To wean them from the influence of that personal competition in a commercial society which leads to sordid aims. To place before them the unsatisfied want of the uneasy and distressed multitude, and to breathe into them the charity which seeks to heal its mental and moral diseases. We were led to select premises at Battersea chiefly on account of the very frank and cordial welcome with which the suggestion of our plans was received by the Hon. and Rev. Robert Eden, the vicar of Battersea. Mr. Eden offered the use of his village schools in aid of the training school, as the sphere in which the pupils might obtain a practical acquaintance with the art of instruction. He also undertook to superintend the training school in all that related to religion. . . .

The great natural records of Switzerland, and its historical recollections, abound with subjects for instructive commentary, of which the professors of the Normal Schools avail themselves in their autumnal excursions with their pupils. The natural features of the country; its drainage, soils, agriculture; the causes which have affected the settlement of its inhabitants and its institutions; the circumstances which have assisted in the formation of the national character, and have thus made the history of their country, are more clearly apprehended by lessons gathered in the presence of facts typical of other facts scattered over hill and valley. England is so rich in historical recollections, and in the monuments by which the former periods of her history are linked with the present time, that it would seem to be a not unimportant duty of the educator to avail himself of such facts as lie within the range of his observation, in order that the historical knowledge of his scholar may be associated with these records, marking the progress of civilisation in his native country. Few schools are placed beyond the reach of such means of instruction. Where they do not exist, the country must present some natural features worthy of being perused. These should not be neglected.

In book-learning there is always a danger that the thing signified may not be discerned through the sign. The child may acquire words instead of thoughts. To have a clear and earnest conviction of the reality of the things signified, the object of the child's instruction should as frequently as possible be brought under its eye. Thus Pestalozzi was careful to devise lessons on objects in which, by actual contact with the sense, the children were led to discern qualities which they afterwards described in words. Such lessons have no meaning to persons who are satisfied with instruction by rote. But we contend that it is important to a right moral state of the intelligence that the child should have a clear perception and *vivid conviction* of every fact presented to its mind. We are of opinion that to extend the province of faith and implicit unreasoning obedience to those subjects which are the proper objects on which the perceptive faculties ought to be exercised, and on which the reason should be employed, is to undermine the basis of an unwavering faith in revelation, by provoking the rebellion of the human spirit against authority in matters in which reason is free.

To the young, the truth (bare before the sight, palpable to the touch, embodied in forms which the senses realise) has a charm which no mere words can convey, until they are recognised as the sign of the truth, which the mind comprehends. In all that relates to the external phenomena of the world, the best book is nature, with an intelligent interpreter. What concerns the social state of man may be best apprehended after lessons in the fields, the ruins, the mansions, and the streets within the range of the school. Lessons on the individual objects prepare the mind for generalizations, and for the exercise of faith in its proper province. Elementary schools, in which word-teaching only exists, do not produce earnest and truthful

men. The practice, prevalent in certain parts of the High-
lands and Wales, of teaching the children to read English
books, though they understand nothing of the English
language, is about as reasonable as the ordinary mode of
teaching by rote, either matters which the children do
not understand, or which they do not receive with a lively
conviction of their truth. The master who neglects opportunities of satisfying the intelligence of his pupil on anything that can be made obvious to the sense, must be
content to find that when his lessons rise to abstractions
he will be gazed upon by vacant faces. The mind will
refuse a lively confidence in general truths, when it has
not been convinced of the existence of the particular facts
from which they are derived. From a master, accustomed
to regard himself as the interpreter of nature, as the en-
grafter of thoughts and not of words, and who is endeav-
ouring to form the character of his pupils by inspiring
them with an earnest love for truth, the pupils will gladly
take much upon authority with a lively confidence. From
the rote teacher they take nothing but words; he gains no
confidence; it is difficult to love him, because it is not
obvious what good he communicates; it is difficult to trust
him, because he asks belief when he takes no pains to
inspire conviction. What reverence can attach to a man
teaching a Highland child to read English words, which
are unmeaning sounds to him?

The excursions of the directors of the Swiss Normal
Schools also serve the purpose of breaking for a time an
almost conventual seclusion, which forms a characteristic
of establishments in which the education of the habits,
as well as the instruction of the intelligence, is kept in
view. These excursions in Switzerland extend to several
days, and even longer in schools of the more wealthy
classes. The pupils are thus thrown in contact with actual

society; their resources are taxed by the incidents of each day; their moral qualities are somewhat tried, and they obtain a glimpse of the perspective of their future life. It is not only important in this way to know what the condition of society is before the pupil is required to enter it, but it is also necessary to keep constantly before his eye the end and aim of education—that it is a preparation for the duties of his future life, and to understand in what respect each department of his studies is adapted to prepare him for the actual performance of those duties. For each class of society there is an appropriate education. The Normal Schools of Switzerland are founded on this principle. None are admitted who are not devoted to the vocation of masters of elementary schools. The three or four years of their residence in the school are considered all too short for a complete preparation for these functions. The time therefore is consumed in appropriate studies, care being taken that these studies are so conducted as to discipline and develope the intelligence; to form habits of thought and action; and to inspire the pupil with principles on which he may repose in the discharge of his duties.

Among these studies and objects, the actual condition of the labouring class, its necessities, resources, and intelligence, form a most important element. The teachers go forth to observe for themselves; they come back to receive further instruction from their master. They are led to anticipate their own relations to the commune or parish in which their future school will be placed. They are prepared by instruction to fulfil certain of the communal duties which may usefully devolve upon them; such as registrar, precentor, or leader of the church choir, and clerk to the associations of the village. They receive familiar expositions of the law affecting the fulfilment of these duties.

The benefits derived from these arrangements are great; not only in furnishing these rural communes with men competent to the discharge of their duties, but the anticipations of future utility, and the conviction that their present studies enfold the germ of their future life, gives an interest to their pursuits, which it would be difficult to communicate, if the sense of their importance were more vague and indistinct.

To this end, in the excursions from Battersea we have been careful to enter the schools on our route, and lessons have been given on the duties attaching to the offices which may be properly discharged by a village schoolmaster in connexion with his duty of instructing the young. . . .

In proceeding to speak of the intellectual training, we premise that this report affords little opportunity for an explanation of the principles which have determined and regulated the preparatory course of instruction, and that we do not intend to anticipate the course which will be pursued in the future periods of study for the certificates of *Scholar* and *Master*. The questions which beset every step of this path could only be properly discussed in a work on pedagogy, resembling the numerous German publications on this subject. Brief hints only of these principles can find a place in the remarks we have to offer on the preparatory course.

The students have been stimulated in their application by a constant sense of the practical utility of their intellectual labours. After morning prayers, they are from day to day reminded of the connexion between their present and future pursuits, and informed how every part of the discipline and study has a direct relation to the duties of a schoolmaster. The conviction thus created becomes a powerful incentive to exertion, which might be wanting if those studies were selected only because they were important as a discipline of the mind.

The sense of practical utility seems as important to the earnestness of the student as the lively conviction attending object teaching in the early and simplest form of elementary instruction. In the earliest steps an acquaintance with the real is necessary to lively conceptions of truth, and at a later period a sense of the value of knowledge resulting from *experience* inspires the strongest conviction of the dignity and importance of all truth, where its immediate practical utility is not obvious.

Far, therefore, from fearing that the sense of the practical utility of these studies will lead the students to measure the value of all truth by a low standard, their pursuits have been regulated by the conviction, that the most certain method of attaining a strong sense of the value of truths, not readily applicable to immediate use, is to ascertain by experience the importance of those which can be readily measured by the standard of practical utility. Thus we approach the conception of the momentum of a planet moving in its orbit, from ascertaining the momentum of bodies whose weight and velocity we can measure by the simplest observations. From the level of the experience of the practical utility of certain common truths, the mind gradually ascends to the more abstract, whose importance hence becomes more easily apparent, though their present application is not obvious, and in this way the thoughts most safely approach the most difficult abstractions.

In the humble pursuits of the preparatory course, a lively sense of the utility of their studies has likewise been maintained by the method of instruction adopted. Nothing has been taught *dogmatically,* but everything by the combination of the simplest elements: *i.e.,* the course which a discoverer must have trod has been followed, and the way in which truths have been ascertained pointed out by a synthetical demonstration of each successive step. The labour of the previous analysis of the subject is the duty of the teacher, and is thus removed from the child.

The preparatory course is especially important, because the pupil's instruction is conducted on the principles which will guide him in the management of his own school. Having ascertained what the pupil knows, the teacher endeavours to lead him by gentle and easy steps from the known to the unknown. The instruction, in the whole preparatory course, is chiefly oral, and is illustrated, as much as possible, by appeals to nature and by demonstrations. Books are not resorted to until the teacher is convinced that the mind of his pupil is in a state of healthful activity; that there has been awakened in him a lively interest in truth, and that he has become acquainted practically with the inductive method of acquiring knowledge. At this stage the rules, the principles of which have been orally communicated, and with whose application he is familiar, are committed to memory from books, to serve as a means of recalling more readily the knowledge and skill thus attained. This course is Pestalozzian, and, it will be perceived, is the reverse of the method usually followed, which consists in giving the pupil the rule first. Experience, however, has confirmed us in the superiority of the plan we have pursued. Sometimes a book, as for example a work on Physical Geography, is put into his hands, in order that it may be carefully read, and that the student may prepare himself to give before the class a verbal abstract of the chapter selected for this purpose, and to answer such questions as may be proposed to him, either by the tutor or by his fellows. During the preparatory course exercises of this kind have not been so numerous as they will be in the more advanced stages of instruction. Until habits of attention and steady application had been formed, it seemed undesirable to allow to the pupils hours for self-sustained study, or voluntary occupation. Constant superintendence is necessary to the formation of correct habits, in these and in all other respects, in the preparatory course. The entire day is therefore occupied with a succession of engagements in household work and out-door labour, devotional exercises, meals, and instruction. Recreation is sought in change of employment. These changes afford such pleasure, and the sense of utility and duty is so constantly maintained, that recreation in the ordinary sense is not needed. Leisure from such occupations is never sought excepting to write a letter to a friend, or occasionally to visit some near relative. The pupils all present an air of cheerfulness. They proceed from one lesson to another, and to their several occupations, with an elasticity of mind which affords the best proof that the mental and physical effects of the training are auspicious.

In the early steps towards the formation of correct habits, it is necessary that (until the power of self-guidance is obtained) the pupil should be constantly under the eye of a master, not disposed to exercise authority so much as to give assistance and advice. Before the habit of self-direction is formed, it is therefore pernicious to leave much time at the disposal of the pupil. Proper intellectual and moral aims must be inspired, and the pupil must attain a knowledge of the mode of employing his time with skill, usefully, and under the guidance of right motives, ere he can be properly left to the spontaneous suggestions of his own mind. Here, therefore, the moral and the intellectual training are in the closest harmony. The formation of correct habits, and the growth of right sentiments, ought to precede such confidence in the pupil's powers of self-direction as is implied in leaving him either much time unoccupied, or in which his labours are not under the immediate superintendence of his teacher.

In the preparatory course, therefore, the whole time is employed under superintendence, but towards the close of the course a gradual trial of the pupil's powers of self-guidance is commenced; first, by intrusting him with certain studies unassisted by the teacher. Those who zealously and successfully employ their time will, by degrees, be intrusted with a greater period for self-sustained intellectual or physical exertion. Further evidence of the existence of the proper qualities will lead to a more liberal confidence, until habits of application and the power of pursuing their studies successfully, and without assistance, are attained.

The subjects of the preparatory course were strictly rudimental. It will be found that the knowledge obtained in the elementary schools now in existence is a very meager preparation for the studies of a training school for teachers. Until the elementary schools are improved it will be found necessary to go to the very roots of all knowledge, and to re-arrange such knowledge as the pupils have attained, in harmony with the principles on which they must ultimately communicate it to others. Many of our pupils enter the school with the broadest provincial dialect, scarcely able to read with fluency and precision, much less with ease and expression. Some were ill-furnished with the commonest rules of arithmetic, and wrote clumsily and slowly.

They have been made acquainted with the *phonic*

method of teaching to read practised in Germany. Their defects of pronunciation have been corrected to a large extent by the adoption of this method, and by means of deliberate and emphatic syllabic reading, in a well sustained and correct tone. The principles on which the *laut* or *phonic* method depends have been explained at considerable length as a part of the course of lessons on method which has been communicated to them, and they will commence the practice of this method in the village school as soon as the lesson-books now in course of printing are published.

We have deemed it of paramount importance that they should acquire a thorough knowledge of the elements and structure of the English language. The lessons in reading were in the first place made the means of leading them to an examination of the structure of sentences, and practical oral lessons were given on grammar and etymology according to the method pursued by Mr. Wood in the Edinburgh Sessional School. The results of these exercises were tested by the lessons of dictation and of composition which accompanied the early stages of this course, and by which a lively sense of the utility of a knowledge of grammatical construction and of the etymological relations of words was developed. As soon as this feeling was created, the oral instruction in grammar assumed a more positive form. The theory on which the rules were founded was explained, and the several laws when well understood were dictated in the least exceptionable formulae, and were written out and committed to memory. In this way they proceeded through the whole of the theory and rules of grammar before they were intrusted with any book on the subject, lest they should depend for their knowledge on a mere effort of the memory to retain a formula not well understood.

At each stage of their advance, corresponding exercises were resorted to, in order to familiarise them with the application of the rules.

When they had in this way passed through the ordinary course of grammatical instruction, they were intrusted with books, to enable them to give the last degree of precision to their conceptions.

In etymology the lessons were in like manner practical and oral. They were first derived from the reading-lessons of the day, and applied to the exercises and examinations accompanying the course, and after a certain progress had been made, their further advance was insured by systematic lessons from books.

A course of reading in English literature, by which the taste may be refined by an acquaintance with the best models of style, and with those authors whose works have exercised the most beneficial influence on the mind of this nation, has necessarily been postponed to another part of the course. It, however, forms one of the most important elements in the conception of the objects to be attained in a training school, that the teacher should be inspired with a discriminating but earnest admiration for those gifts of great minds to English literature which are alike the property of the peasant and the peer; national treasures which are among the most legitimate sources of national feelings.

A thorough acquaintance with the English language can alone make the labouring class accessible to the best influence of English civilisation. Without this, lettered men will find it difficult, if not impossible, to teach the vulgar.

Those who have had close intercourse with the labouring classes well know with what difficulty they comprehend words not of a Saxon origin, and how frequently addresses to them are unintelligible from the continual use of terms of a Latin or Greek derivation; yet the daily language of the middle and upper classes abounds with such words; many of the formularies of our church are full of them, and hardly a sermon is preached which does not in every page contain numerous examples of their use. Phrases of this sort are so naturalised in the language of the educated classes, that entirely to omit them has the appearance of pedantry and baldness, and even disgusts persons of taste and refinement. Therefore, in addressing a mixed congregation, it seems impossible to avoid using them, and the only mode of meeting the inconvenience alluded to is to instruct the humbler classes in their meaning. The method we have adopted for this purpose has been copied from that first introduced in the Edinburgh Sessional Schools; every compound word is analysed, and the separate meaning of each member pointed out, so that, at present, there are few words in the English language which our pupils cannot thoroughly comprehend, and from their acquaintance with the common roots and principles of etymology, the new compound terms, which the demands of civilisation are daily introducing, are almost immediately understood by them. We believe that there are few acquirements more conducive to clearness of thought, or that can be more usefully introduced into common schools, than a thorough knowledge of the English language, and that the absence of it gives power to the illiterate teacher and demagogue, and deprives the lettered man of his just influence.

Similar remarks might be extended to style. It is equally obvious that the educated use sentences of a construction presenting difficulties to the vulgar which are frequently almost insurmountable. It is, therefore, not only necessary that the meaning of words should be taught on a logical system in our elementary schools, but that the children should be made familiar with extracts from our best authors on subjects suited to their capacity. It cannot be permitted to remain the opprobrium of this country that its greatest minds have bequeathed their thoughts to the nation in a style at once pure and simple, but still inaccessible to the intelligence of the great body of the people. . . .

In like manner, in *arithmetic* it has been deemed desirable to put them in possession of the pre-eminently synthetical method of Pestalozzi. As soon as the requisite tables and series of lessons, analysed to the simplest elements, could be procured, the principles on which complex numerical combinations rest were rendered familiar to them, by leading the pupils through the earlier course of Pestalozzi's lessons on numbers, from simple unity to compound fractional quantities; connecting with them the series of exercises in mental arithmetic which they are so well calculated to introduce and to illustrate. The use of such a method dispels the gloom which might attend the most expert use of the common rules of arithmetic, and which commonly afford the pupil little light to guide his steps off the beaten path illuminated by the rule.

The analysis in the lessons of Pestalozzi is so minute as to inspire all minds, who have attained a certain knowledge of number by other means, with a doubt whether time may not be lost by tracing all the minute steps of the analytical series over which his lessons pass. The opposite practice of dogmatic teaching is so ruinous, however, to the intellectual habits, and so imperfect a means of developing the intelligence, that it ought, we think, at all expense of time, to be avoided. With this conviction, the method of Pestalozzi has been diligently pursued.

Whilst these lessons have been in progress, the common

rules of arithmetic have been examined by the light of this method. Their theory has been explained, and by constant practice the pupils have been led to acquire expertness in them, as well as to pursue the common principles on which they rest, and to ascertain the practical range within which each rule ought to be employed. The ordinary lessons on mental arithmetic have taken their place in the course of instruction separately from the peculiar rules which belong to Pestalozzi's series.

These lessons also prepared the pupils for proceeding at an early period in a similar manner with the elements of algebra, and with practical lessons in mensuration and land surveying.

These last subjects were considered of peculiar importance, as comprising one of the most useful industrial developments of a knowledge of the laws of number. Unless, in elementary schools, the instruction proceed beyond the knowledge of abstract rules, to their actual application to the practical necessities of life, the scholar will have little interest in his studies, because he will not perceive their importance, and, moreover, when he leaves the school, they will be of little use, because he has not learned to apply his knowledge to any purpose. On this account boys, who have been educated in common elementary schools, are frequently found, in a few years after they have left, to have forgotten the greater part even of the slender amount of knowledge they had acquired.

The use of arithmetic to the carpenter, the builder, the labourer, and artisan, ought to be developed by teaching mensuration and land surveying in elementary schools. If the scholars do not remain long enough to attain so high a range, the same principle should be applied to every step of their progress. The practical application of the simplest rules should be shown by familiar examples.

As soon as the child can count, he should be made to count objects, such as money, the figures on the face of a clock, &c. When he can add, he should have before him shop-bills, accounts of the expenditure of earnings, accounts of wages. In every arithmetical rule similar useful exercises are a part of the art of a teacher, whose sincere desire is to fit his pupil for the application of his knowledge to the duties of life, the preparation for which should be always suggested to the pupil's mind as a powerful incentive to action. These future duties should be always placed in a cheering and hopeful point of view. The mere repetition of a table of numbers has less of education in it than a drill in the *balance-step*.

Practical instruction in the *book-keeping* necessary for the management of the household was for these reasons given to those who acted as stewards; accounts were kept of the seeds, manure, and garden produce, &c., as preparatory to a course of book-keeping, which will follow.

The recently rapid development of the industry and commerce of this country by machinery creates a want for well-instructed mechanics, which in the present state of education it will be difficult adequately to supply. The steam-engines which drain our coal-fields and mineral veins and beds, which whirl along every railroad, which toil on the surface of every river, and issue from every estuary, are committed to the charge of men of some practical skill, but of mean education. The mental resources of the classes who are practically intrusted with the guidance of this great development of national power should not be left uncultivated. This new force has grown rapidly, in consequence of the genius of the people, and the natural resources of this island, and in spite of their ignorance. But our supremacy at sea, and our manufacturing and commercial prosperity (inseparable elements) depend on the successful progress of those arts by which our present position has been attained.

On this account we have deemed inseparable from the education of a schoolmaster a knowledge of the *elements of mechanics* and of the laws of heat, sufficient to enable him to explain the structure of the various kinds of steam-engines in use in this country. This instruction has proved one of the chief features even of the preparatory course, as we feared that some of the young men might leave the establishment as soon as they had obtained the certificates of candidates, and we were unwilling that they should go forth without some knowledge at least of one of the chief elements of our national prosperity, or altogether without power to make the working man acquainted with the great agent, which has had more influence on the destiny of the working classes than any other single fact in our history, and which is probably destined to work still greater changes.

Knowledge and national prosperity are here in strict alliance. Not only do the arts of peace—the success of our trade—our power to compete with foreign rivals—our safety on our railways and in our steam-ships—depend on the spread of this knowledge, but the future defence of this country from foreign aggression can only result from our being superior to every nation in those arts. The schoolmaster is an agent despised at present, but whose importance for the attainment of this end will, by the results of a few years, be placed in bold relief before the public. . . .

Physical geography has been deemed the true basis of all instruction in the geography of industry and commerce, which ought to form the chief subject of geographical instruction in elementary schools. The tutor has first endeavoured to convince the pupils that nothing which presents itself to the eye in a well-drawn map is to be regarded as accidental; the boldness of the promontories; the deep indenture of the bays; the general bearings of the coast; are all referable to natural laws. In these respects the eastern and western coasts of England are in striking contrast, in appearance, character, and in the circumstances which occasion their peculiarities. The physical geography of England commences with a description of the elevation of the mountain ranges, the different levels, and the drainage of the country. The course, rapidity, and volume of the rivers are referable to the elevation and extent of the country which they drain. From the climate, levels, and drainage, with little further matter, the agricultural tracts of the country may be indicated; and when the great coal-fields and the mineral veins and beds, the depth of the bays and rivers, are known, the distribution of the population is found to be in strict relation to certain natural laws. Even the ancient political divisions of the country are, on inspection, found to be in close dependence on its drainage. The counties are river basins, which were the first seats of tribes of population. If any new political distribution were to be made, it would necessarily, in like manner, be affected by some natural law, which it is equally interesting and useful to trace.

Geography taught in this way is a constant exercise to the reasoning powers. The pupil is led to trace the mutual dependence of facts, which, in ordinary instruction, are taught as the words of a vocabulary. Geography taught in the ordinary way is as reasonable an acquisition as the catalogue of a museum, which a student might be compelled to learn as a substitute for natural history. A catalogue of towns, rivers, bays, promontories, &c., is even less geography than the well-arranged catalogue of a museum is natural history, because the classification has a logical meaning in the latter case, which is absent in the former. . . .

Some of the reasons inducing us to attach much importance to the cultivation of *vocal music* have already been briefly indicated. We regarded it as a powerful auxiliary in rendering the devotional services of the household, of the parish church, and of the village school solemn and impressive. Our experience satisfies us that we by no means over-estimated this advantage, though all the results are not yet obtained which, we trust, will flow from the right use of these means.

Nor were we indifferent to the cheerfulness diffused in schools by the singing of those melodies which are attractive to children, nor unconscious of the moral power which music has when linked with sentiments which it is the object of education to inspire. We regard school songs as an important means of diffusing a cheerful view of the duties of a labourer's life; of diffusing joy and honest pride over English industry. Therefore, to neglect so powerful a moral agent in elementary education as vocal music would appear to be unpardonable. We availed ourselves of some arrangements which were at this time in progress, under the superintendence of the Committee of Council, for the introduction of the method of M. Wilhem, which has been singularly successful in France. It affords us great satisfaction to say how much advantage the pupils of the Training School have derived from the instruction they have received, during the development of this method, from Mr. Hullah, the gentleman selected by the Committee of Council to adapt the method of Wilhem, under their superintendence, to the tastes and habits of the English people. Mr. Hullah has devoted himself with unceasing assiduity and great skill to this important public duty; and his pupils will always remember, with a pleasure without any alloy, the delight-ful lessons they have received from him.

The method of Wilhem is simply an application of the Pestalozzian method of ascending from the simple to the general through a clearly analysed series, in which every step of the progress is distinctly marked, and enables the pupil, without straining his faculties, to arrive at results which might otherwise have been difficult of attainment. Wilhem has not in any respect deviated from the well-ascertained results of experience, either in the theory of music or in the musical signs; but he has with great skill arranged all the early lessons, so as to smooth the path of the student to the desirable result of being able to read music with ease, and to sing with skill and expression even difficult music at sight. The progress of the pupils at Battersea has been very gratifying, and, even in the brief period which has elapsed since the opening of the school, they sing music at sight with considerable facility.

SOURCE: *Four Periods,* pp. 295–300, 303–304, 307–309, 319–323, 333–346, 353–355.

4

Second Report on the Schools for the Training of Parochial Schoolmasters at Battersea

(1843)

In this Report, written jointly with E. C. Tufnell, Kay-Shuttleworth announces the transfer of the training schools at Battersea, which they had been operating with their own funds, to the National Society. Battersea thereby became an integral part of the teacher training system which Kay-Shuttleworth was to invigorate and bring under state control in 1846. The transfer symbolizes the continuity between the poor law and denominational schools of the early Victorian period and the new forms of popular education which he was trying to establish. Kay-Shuttleworth's observations on the status of teachers in this Report reflect the conservative and traditionalist strain in his thought. They stand out in contrast to the more positive conception of the position of the elementary school teacher that was to underlie his policies in 1846.

. . . The main object of a Normal School is the *formation of the character of the schoolmaster*. This was the

primary idea which guided our earliest efforts in the establishment of the Battersea Schools on a basis different from
that of any previous example in this country. We have submitted to your Lordship the reasons which have led us to
modify one of the chief features of our plan, but our
convictions adhere with undiminished force to the principle on which the schools were originally founded. They
were intended to be an institution, in which every object
was subservient to the *formation of the character of the
schoolmaster,* as an intelligent Christian man entering on
the instruction of the poor, with religious devotion to his
work. If we propose to change the means, the end we have
in view is the same. Compelled by the foregoing considerations to think the course of training we proposed for
youths does not prepare them for the charge of large
schools in manufacturing towns, we are anxious that the
system pursued in Holland should be adopted, as a training preparatory to the examination of the pupil teachers
previously to their admission into a Normal School.
Finding that the patrons of students and the friends of
the establishment are unable, for the most part, to support a longer training for young men than one year and a
half, we are more anxious respecting the investigation of
their previous characters and connections, and more
fastidious as to their intellectual qualifications and acquirements. . . .

The impression produced upon the characters of the
students during their residence is of paramount importance.

They are commonly selected from a humble sphere.
They are the sons of small tradesmen, of bailiffs, of servants, or of superior mechanics. Few have received any
education, except that given in a common parochial
school. They read and write very imperfectly; are unable

to indite a letter correctly; and are seldom skilful, even in the first four rules of arithmetic. Their biblical knowledge is meagre and inaccurate, and all their conceptions, not less on religious than on other subjects, are vague and confused, even when they are not also very limited or erroneous. Their habits have seldom prepared them for the severely regular life of the Normal School, much less for the strenuous effort of attention and application required by the daily routine of instruction. Such concentration of the mind would soon derange the health, if the course of training did not provide moderate daily exercise in the garden, at proper intervals. The mental torpor, which at first is an obstacle to improvement, generally passes away in about three months, and from that period the student makes rapid progress in the studies of the school. The tables and examination papers appended to Mr. Allen's Report show the state of the pupil's acquirements, and how his intellectual powers are strengthened, when his course of instruction is completed.

These attainments, humble though they be, might prove dangerous to the character of the student, if his intellectual development were the chief concern of the masters.

How easy it would be for him to form an overweening estimate of his knowledge and ability, must be apparent, when it is remembered that he will measure his learning by the standard of that possessed by his own friends and neighbours. He will find himself suddenly raised by a brief course of training to the position of a teacher and example. If his mind were not thoroughly penetrated by a religious principle, or if a presumptuous or mercenary tone had been given to his character, he might go forth to bring discredit upon education by exhibiting a precocious vanity, an insubordinate spirit, or a selfish ambition.

He might become not the gentle and pious guide of the children of the poor, but a hireling into whose mind had sunk the doubts of the sceptic; in whose heart was the worm of social discontent; and who had changed the docility of ignorance and dulness, for the restless impatience of a vulgar and conceited sciolist.

In the formation of the character of the schoolmaster, the discipline of the Training School should be so devised as to prepare him for the modest respectability of his lot. He is to be a Christian teacher, following him who said, "he that will be my disciple, let him take up his cross." Without the spirit of self-denial, he is nothing. His reward must be in his work. There should be great simplicity in the life of such a man.

Obscure and secluded schools need masters of a contented spirit, to whom the training of the children committed to their charge, has charms sufficient to concentrate their thoughts and exertions on the humble sphere in which they live, notwithstanding the privations of a life but little superior to the level of the surrounding peasantry. When the scene of the teacher's exertions is in a neighbourhood which brings him into association with the middle and upper classes of society, his emoluments will be greater, and he will be surrounded by temptations which, in the absence of a suitable preparation of mind, might rob him of that humility and gentleness, which are among the most necessary qualifications of the teacher of a common school.

In the Training School, habits should be formed consistent with the modesty of his future life. On this account we attach peculiar importance to the discipline which we have established at Battersea. Only one servant, besides a cook, has been kept for the domestic duties of the household. From the table contained in Mr. Allen's Report, you will perceive that the whole household work, with the exception of the scouring of the floors and cooking, is performed by the students, and they likewise not only milk and clean the cows, feed and tend the pigs, but have charge of the stores, wait upon each other, and cultivate the garden. We cannot too emphatically state our opinion that no portion of this work could be omitted, without a proportionate injury to that contentment of spirit, without which the character of the student is liable to be overgrown with the errors we have described. He has to be prepared for a humble and subordinate position, and though master of his school, to his scholars he is to be a parent, and to his superiors an intelligent servant and minister.

The garden work also serves other important ends. Some exercise and recreation from the scholastic labours are indispensable. Nevertheless, a large portion of the day cannot be devoted to it, and when three or four hours only can be spared, care should be taken that the whole of this time is occupied by moderate and healthful exertion in the open air. A period of recreation employed according to the discretion of the students would be liable to abuse. It might often be spent in listless sauntering, or in violent exertion. Or if a portion of the day were thus withdrawn from the observation of the masters of the school, it would prove a period in which associations might be formed among the students inconsistent with the discipline; and habits might spring up to counteract the influence of the instruction and admonition of the masters. In so brief a period of training, it is necessary that the entire conduct of the student should be guided by a superior mind.

Not only by the daily labour of the garden, are the health and morals of the school influenced, but habits are formed consistent with the student's future lot. It is well both for his own health, and for the comfort of his family, that the schoolmaster should know how to grow his garden stuff, and should be satisfied with innocent recreation near his home.

We have also adhered to the frugal diet which we at first selected for the school. Some little variety has been introduced, but we attach great importance to the students being accustomed to a diet so plain and economical, and to arrangements in their dormitories so simple and devoid of luxury, that in after life they will not in a humble school be visited with a sense of privation, when their scanty fare and mean furniture are compared with the more abundant food and comforts of the training school. We have therefore met every rising complaint respecting either the quantity or quality of the food, or the humble accommodation in the dormitories, with explanations of the importance of forming, in the school, habits of frugality, and of the paramount duty of nurturing a patient spirit, to meet the future privations of the life of a teacher of the poor. Though we have admitted some variety into the ingredients of the diet, we have not increased the quantity, or raised the quality, of the food of the school, or added one element even of additional comfort to their life.

Our experience also leads us to attach much importance to simplicity and propriety of dress. For the younger pupils we had, on this account, prepared a plain dark dress of rifle green, and a working dress of fustian cord. As respects the adults, we have felt the importance of checking the slightest tendency to peculiarity of dress, lest it should degenerate into foppery. We have endeavoured to impress on the students that the dress and the manners of a master of a School for the poor should be decorous, but that the prudence of his life should likewise find expression in their simplicity. There should be no habit nor external sign of self-indulgence or vanity.

On the other hand, the master is to be prepared for a life of laborious exertion. He must, therefore, form habits of early rising, and of activity and persevering industry. In the winter, before it is light, the household work must be finished, and the school-rooms prepared by the students for the duties of the day. One hour and a half is thus occupied. After this work is accomplished, one class must assemble winter and summer, at a quarter to seven o'clock, for instruction. The day is filled with the claims of duty requiring the constant exertion of mind and body, until at half-past nine the household retire to rest.

By this laborious and frugal life, economy of management is reconciled with the efficiency both of the moral and intellectual training of the School, and the master goes forth into the world humble, industrious, and instructed.

But into the student's character higher sentiments must enter, if we rightly conceive the mission of the master of a school for the poor. On the religious condition of the household, under the blessing of God, depends the cultivation of that religious feeling, without which the spirit of self-sacrifice cannot take its right place among the motives which ought to form the mainspring of a schoolmaster's activity.

There is a necessity for incessant vigilance in the management of a training school. The Principal should be *wise as a serpent,* while the gentleness of his discipline, and his affectionate solicitude for the well-being of his pupils, should encourage the most unreserved communications with him. Much of his leisure should be devoted to private interviews with the students, and employed in instilling into their minds high principles of action. A cold and repulsive air of authority may preserve the appearance of order, regularity, and submission in the household; but these will prove delusive signs if the Principal does not possess the respect and confidence, not to say the affections, of his charge. He should be most accessible, and unwearied in the patience with which he listens to confessions and inquiries. While it is felt to be impossible that he should enter into any compromise with evil, there should be no such severity in his tone of rebuke as to check that confidence which seeks guidance from a superior intelligence. As far as its relation to the Principal only is concerned, every fault should be restrained and corrected by a conviction of the pain and anxiety which it causes to an anxious friend, rather than by the fear of a too jealous authority. Thus conscience will gradually be roused by the example of a master, respected for his purity, and loved for his gentleness, and inferior sentiments will be replaced by motives derived from the highest source.

Where so much has to be learned, and where, among other studies, so much religious knowledge must be acquired, there is danger that religion should be regarded chiefly as a subject for the exercise of the intellect. A speculative religious knowledge, without those habits and feelings which are the growth of deeply-seated religious convictions, may be a dangerous acquisition to a teacher of the young. How important, therefore, is it, that the religious services of the household should become the means of cultivating a spirit of devotion, and that the religious instruction of the School should be so conducted as not merely to inform the memory, but to master the convictions and to interest the feelings. Religion is not merely to be taught in the School—it must be the element in which the students live.

This religious life is to be nurtured by the example, by the public instruction of the Principal, and by his private counsel and admonition; by the religious services of the household; by the personal intercourse of the students, and the habits of private meditation and devotion which they are led to form; by the public worship of the church, and by the acts of charity and self-denial which belong to their future calling.

How important is it that the Principal should embody such an example of purity and elevation of character, of gentleness of manners and of unwearied benevolence, as to increase the power of his teaching, by the respect and conviction which wait upon a consistent life. Into the religious services of the household, he should endeavour to inspire such a spirit of devotion as would spread itself through the familiar life, and hallow every season of retirement. The management of the village school affords opportunities for cultivating habits of kindness and patience. The students should be instructed in the organisation and conduct of Sunday schools; they should be trained in the preparation of the voluntary teachers by previous instruction; in the visitation of the absent children; in the management of the clothing and sick clubs and libraries attached to such schools. They should be accustomed to the performance of those parochial duties in which the schoolmaster may lighten the burthen of the clergyman. For this purpose they should learn to keep the accounts of the benefit club. They should instruct and manage the village choir, and should learn to play the organ.

While in attendance on the village school, it is peculiarly important that they should accompany the master in his visits to children detained at home by sickness, and should listen to the words of counsel and comfort which he may then administer; they should also attend him when his duty requires a visit to the parents of some refractory or indolent scholar, and should learn how to secure their aid in the correction of the faults of the child.

Before he leaves the Training School, the student should have formed a distinct conception, from precept and practice, how his example, his instruction, and his works of charity and religion, ought to promote the Christian civilisation of the community in which he labours.

Turn we again to the contrast of such a picture. Let us suppose a school in which this vigilance in the formation of character is deemed superfluous; or a Principal, the guileless simplicity of whose character is not strengthened by the wisdom of experience. A fair outward show of order and industry, and great intellectual development, may, in either case, be consistent, with the latent progress of a rank corruption of manners, mining all beneath. Unless the searching intelligence of the Principal is capable of discerning the dispositions of his charge, and anticipating their tendencies, he is unequal to the task of moulding the minds of his pupils, by the power of a loftier character and a superior will. In that case, or when the Principal deems such vigilance superfluous and is content with the intellectual labours of his office, leaving the little republic, of which he is the head, to form its own manners, and to create its own standard of principle and action, the catastrophe of a deep ulcerous corruption, is not likely to be long delayed.

In either case it is easy to trace the progress of degeneracy. A school, in which the formation of character is not the chief aim of the masters, must abandon that all-important end to the republic of scholars. When these are selected from the educated, and upper ranks of society, the school will derive its code of morals from that prevalent in such classes. When the pupils belong to a very humble class, their characters are liable, under such arrangements, to be compounded of the ignorance, coarseness, and vices of the lowest orders. One pupil, the victim of low vices, or of a vulgar coarseness of thought, escaping the eye of an unsuspicious Principal, or unsought for by the vigilance which is expended on the intellectual progress of the school, may corrupt the private intercourse of the students with low buffoonery, profligate jests, and sneers at the self-denying zeal of the humble student; may gradually lead astray one after another of the pupils to clandestine habits, if not to the secret practice of vice. Under such circumstances, the counsels of the Principal would gradually become subjects of ridicule. A conspiracy of direct insubordination would be formed. The influence of the Superior would barely maintain a fair external appearance of order and respect.

Every master issuing from such a school would become the active agent of a degeneracy of manners, by which the humbler ranks of society would be infected.

The formation of the character is, therefore, the chief aim of a Training School, and the Principal should be a man of Christian earnestness, of intelligence, of experience, of knowledge of the world, and of the humblest simplicity and purity of manners.

Next to the formation of the character of the pupil is, in our estimation, the general development of his intelligence. The extent of his attainments, though within a certain range a necessary object of his training, should be subordinate to that mental cultivation, which confers the powers of self-education, and gives the greatest strength to his reflective faculties. On this account, among others, we attach importance to the methods of imparting knowledge pursued in the Normal School. While we have ensured that the attainments of the students should be exact, by testing them with searching examinations, repeated at the close of every week, and reiterated lessons on all subjects in which any deficiency was discovered, nothing has been taught by rote. The memory has never been stored, without the exercise of the reason. Nothing has been learned which has not been understood. This very obvious course is too frequently lost sight of in the humbler branches of learning—principles being hidden in rules, defining only their most convenient application; or buried under a heap of facts, united by no intelligible link. To form the character, to develope the intelligence and to store the mind with the requisite knowledge, these were the objects of the Normal School. . . .

The Battersea Training Schools had been founded with two distinguishing objects:—

1. To give an example of Normal Education for Schoolmasters, comprising the formation of character, the development of the intelligence, appropriate technical instruction, and the acquisition of method and practical skill in conducting an Elementary School.

2. To illustrate the truth that, without violating the rights of conscience, masters trained in a spirit of Christian charity, and instructed in the discipline and doctrines of the Church, might be employed in the mixed schools necessarily connected with public establishments, and in which children of persons of all shades of religious opinion are assembled.

Our first impulse was to remember the generous and unsolicited contributions by which our funds had been replenished, and to turn to those friends who had offered us this voluntary evidence of their sympathy. A little reflection, and the advice of some experienced friends, convinced us that, however successful such an application might be, a subscription for the support of the Schools, in the present agitated state of the public mind, would probably raise a new subject of controversy.

The Training Schools had to a remarkable extent escaped the fierce denunciations with which the success of almost every other effort for the improvement of Elementary Education had been menaced from one or other of the great parties, and we had no desire to expose them to the violence of party feuds, unless it were clear that some signal advantage could thus be obtained for the progress of an efficient religious Education based on the recognition of civil rights. We had no assurance that such an achievement could be won, by the exertions of so fluctuating a body as the subscribers necessary for the support of a charitable institution.

We were unable to fulfil our original design of devoting this establishment to the supply of masters to Schools connected with the executive Government, and especially to the great Schools of Industry for Pauper Children now existing at Norwood, Manchester, Liverpool, Sheffield, and about to be erected elsewhere. We therefore turned to observe in what sphere existed the greatest need of a supply of skilful and religious men, ready to devote their lives to the great work of spreading a truly Christian civilization through the masses of the people. Our personal experience had made us early acquainted with the absence of a growth in the spiritual and intellectual life of the masses, corresponding with the vast material prosperity of the manufacturing districts.

We had witnessed the failure of efforts to found a

scheme of combined Education on the emancipation of infants from the slavery into which the necessities and ignorance of their parents, and the intensity of commercial competition, had sold them.

To arrest the progress of degeneracy towards materialism and sensuality, appeared to us to be the task most worthy of citizens in a nation threatened by corruption from the consequences of ignorance and excessive labour among her lower orders.

It is impossible that the Legislature should, year after year, receive and publish such accounts of the condition of the people as are contained in the Reports of the Hand-loom Weavers' Commission, or of the Commission on the Employment of Women and Children, or that on the Dwellings of the Poor and on the Sanitary Condition of Large Towns, without resolving to confer on the poor some great reward of patience, by offering national security for their future welfare.

These considerations have a general relation, but the state of the manufacturing poor is that which awakens the greatest apprehension. The labour which they undergo is excessive, and they sacrifice their wives and infants to the claims of their poverty, and to the demands of the intense competition of trade. Almost every thing around them tends to materialise and inflame them.

They are assembled in masses—they are exposed to the physical evils arising from the neglect of sanitary precautions, and to the moral contamination of towns—they are accustomed to combine in trades unions and political associations—they are more accessible by agitators, and more readily excited by them.

The time for inquiry into their condition is past, the period for the interference of a sagacious national forethought is at hand. We therefore felt that the imminent risks attending this condition of the manufacturing poor established the largest claim on an institution founded to Educate Christian Teachers for the people.

We have explained the relations which the Training Schools had to the Established Church of this country, and the circumstances by which that condition was determined. When, therefore, we perceived the resources recently collected by the Church to promote the spread of Education in the manufacturing districts, we felt that to contribute towards rendering the Education there provided efficient and comprehensive, was an object strictly consistent with the first of the intentions for which the instruction was founded, and we felt that the force of circumstances had defeated the accomplishment of the second.

After some correspondence with the Bishop of London, we therefore requested the Committee of Council to permit us to transfer the grant made by their Lordships for the enlargement and improvement of the buildings, together with the entire establishment, to the National Society.

SOURCE: *Four Periods,* pp. 399–409, 426–430.

5
Explanation of the Minutes of 1846
(1847)

This pamphlet, published by the Committee of Council on Education, sets forth Kay-Shuttleworth's explanation of the Minutes of 1846, the culmination of his efforts in behalf of popular education. It marked the "third period" in public education, when, under his leadership, the state began to intervene on a large scale.

. . . The authority of Government, especially in a representative system, embodies the national will. There are certain objects too vast, or too complicated, or too important to be intrusted to voluntary associations; they need the assertion of the power, and the application of the resources of the majority. The means for national defence, for the preservation of public order, and the maintenance of the institutions sanctioned by the law; the security of persons and property obtained by the protection of the law and the agency of the police, are among these objects. In like manner the municipal power provides, on principles settled by the legislature, for the regulation of local government, for police and the administration of justice, for the lighting and drainage of our towns, for the supply of water, and for the progressive improvements by which local abuses and defects are removed. These are all objects obviously too vast and too complicated to be accomplished by purely voluntary association. Many of them operate almost solely by restraint or coercion, and some interfere constantly with the individual will—even with the rights of property—and subordinate them to the general advantage. Yet there are persons who sanction a large expenditure by the State for the preservation of public order by the maintenance of the military organisation of the country, for the prevention or detection of crime by the establishment of an almost universally diffused police force, and who regard with complacency the annual outlay on the machinery of criminal jurisprudence, and the secondary punishment offences, yet who deny that the State, which they permit to interfere by penal and coercive arrangements, may apply its resources even to promote the success of voluntary efforts for the education of the people.

To a statesman the condition of the great mass of the people presents a question of the greatest importance and interest. For the security of the life of the humblest wayfarer, the ministers of Queen Elizabeth charged the whole property of the country with a tax for the relief of indigence, which now amounts to five millions per annum. The liberty of the poorest is secured by the same statutes, and defended by the same legal authority as that of the highest. Some signs are beginning to appear that the condition of the poor has attracted the attention of the legislature in the improvement of the discipline of our gaols; in the amelioration of the criminal code; in the mitigation of all punishments, and the limitation of the penalty of death to murder, and a few crimes akin to it; in the attention now paid by Government to the sanitary arrangements of our towns, which has prepared public opinion for the adoption of a legislative arrangement intended to remove pestilence from the habitations of the poor; to promote the cleanliness and comfort of their dwellings, and thus to improve the morality of their households.

These are among the signs that the condition of the common people in England has become, in the opinion of statesmen, one of the chief tests of the prosperity of the nation, and of the stability of public order. The enactments which have restricted the hours of labour of women, children, and young persons in public manufactories, are among the earliest provisions for a great moral reformation intended to reach the condition of the entire body of the working classes. . . .

That it is a function of the legislature to improve domestic morality and household comfort by education is apparent, because on the State devolves the duty of suppressing crime by coercive means and penal enactments. If public order may be preserved by the concerted arrangements of a highly disciplined military organisation, why may not the statesman seek, in the improved intelligence of the people, safeguards, surer and more consistent with personal freedom? Those who would create an alarm at the expenditure required for an efficient system of education, keep out of sight how much the national industry has been obstructed by combinations resulting from ignorance; what has been the cost of military establishments for the protection of society in periods of turbulence—how many millions have been annually expended on those forms of indigence which result from immorality or listless improvidence—how many millions the police force, the machinery of criminal jurisprudence and of secondary punishments engulf—and what is the annual waste in improvident expenditure occasioned by the immoral excesses and crimes of an uneducated people. Those who pretend that public liberty is endangered by the rewards which Government desires to give efficient schoolmasters and their assistants (representing it as the invasion of an army of Government stipendiaries), appear to forget how many thousand troops of the line are employed to protect the institutions of the country—how many thousand police to watch their houses and protect their persons—how many gaolers, warders, and officers of the hulks have charge of the victims of popular ignorance and excess— how many ships are annually freighted with their frightful cargoes to the pandemonium of crime in Van Diemen's land—how many overseers have charge of the convict gangs—and how vast is the outlay which sustains the indigence of orphanage and bastardy, of improvident youth, sensual maturity, and premature age.

The statesman who endeavours to substitute instruction for coercion; to procure obedience to the law by intelligence rather than by fear; to employ a system of encouragement to virtuous exertion, instead of the dark code of penalties against crime; to use the public resources rather in building schools than barracks and convict ships; to replace the constable, the soldier, and the gaoler by the schoolmaster, cannot be justly suspected of any serious design against the liberties of his country, or charged with an improvident employment of the resources of the State.

When, therefore, *freedom of education* from the interference of the Government becomes the war-cry of any party, will it not be suspected that they seek the interest of a class rather than the welfare of the nation; that they prefer popular ignorance to party insignificance; the liberty to neglect the condition of the people, rather than the liberty of progressive civilisation? . . .

By the events which have been thus described, it had been determined that the assistance of Government for the promotion of elementary education should be distributed in aid of voluntary exertions, chiefly in connection with the Church of England and the British and Foreign School Society; with the Church of Scotland, and with those religious communions which united in giving instruction in their schools from the Shorter Catechism of the Assembly of Divines. A new condition was annexed to these grants, viz., that the schools thus aided should be open to inspection by officers appointed by the Crown, but who were not to interfere with the discipline or management of the school, nor even to examine the religious instruction, unless invited by the managers, but only to report the results of their inspection for the information of Parliament and of the public. Two great principles were thus established—the right and duty of the legislature to promote the extension and improvement of elementary education, and the interest of Parliament and the public in the condition of every school aided by the Government. . . .

These arrangements having been made, the application of the Parliamentary Grant to the extension of elementary education proceeded without further interruption. Little could be accomplished in the improvement of the condition of the schools visited, because the Inspectors had no administrative function, for the Parliamentary Grant was then inapplicable to the support of schools; but the publicity given by the Reports of the Inspectors to the condition of elementary education (even in those schools which being recently founded were supported by the most active zeal) tended to bring about a more general acknowledgment of the incompleteness of that instruction which had been dignified with the name of education. The proposal made by the Government, in 1839, to establish a Normal School, awakened public attention to the important influence which such institutions might exert on the character of schoolmasters, and on the standard of instruction throughout the country. Shortly afterwards, a Normal School originated in the exertions of private individuals. This was followed by the establishment of several others, under the auspices of the Church, in London and in other dioceses. The British and Foreign School Society likewise established a Normal School in the Borough Road; and the Church of Scotland, at a later period, one in Edinburgh and another in Glasgow. Eight of these Normal institutions received liberal assistance from the Government for their establishment, who also contributed towards the annual expenses of four of them.

Every new step, however, disclosed the poverty of the resources of the existing system. During the feverish excitement of controversy it was possible, by great exertions, to procure considerable funds for the promotion of education; but with the termination of the conflict, the tendency to personal sacrifices was exhausted, and the original languor returned.

It may be important to trace the consequences of this poverty of resources on the condition of the elementary school, on that of the Normal School, and on the profession of the schoolmaster. These subjects are necessarily so connected, as not to be capable of a separate treatment. The Reports of the Inspectors of Schools disclosed that in a great number of instances, even the primary arrangements for enclosing the school site, providing proper offices, completing the drainage and ventilation of the building, furnishing it with proper means of warmth in winter, and with desks and benches for the scholars, were either executed in a meager and insufficient manner, or were, in some cases, entirely neglected. The schools were generally found ill supplied with the apparatus of instruction; often, the only class-book was the Bible or Testament, desecrated as a horn-book, because indispensable for religious instruction, and on account of the low price at which it is sold by religious associations. If there were any other books, they were often in tatters. Black boards, easels, maps, and other indispensable apparatus of skilful instruction, were seldom to be found, except in the best schools.

The Reports of the Inspectors disclosed a relation between the imperfection of the school and the condition of the schoolmaster of the most painful character. Few efficient elementary schools exist in England, though the number of school-houses has of late years greatly increased. The most prominent of the causes to which these defects are attributable is the fact, that the master of an elementary school is commonly in a position which yields him neither honour nor emolument. He has, therefore, a scanty knowledge even of the humblest rudiments of learning, meager ideas of the duties of his office, and even less skill in their performance.

There is little or nothing in the profession of an elementary schoolmaster, in this country, to tempt a man having a respectable acquaintance with the elements of even humble learning to exchange the certainty of a respectable livelihood in a subordinate condition in trade or commerce, for the mean drudgery of instructing the rude children of the poor in an elementary school, as it is now conducted.

For what is the condition of the master of such a school? He has often an income very little greater than that of an agricultural labourer, and very rarely equal to that of a moderately skilful mechanic. Even this income is to a great degree contingent on the weekly pittances paid from the earnings of his poor neighbours, and liable to be reduced by bad harvests, want of employment, strikes, sickness among the children, or, worst of all, by the calamity of his own ill-health.

Of late years he may more frequently have a small cottage rent-free, but seldom a garden or fuel.

Some portion of his income may be derived from the voluntary subscriptions of the promoters of the school—a precarious source, liable to be dried up by the removal or death of patrons, and the fickleness of friends.

Amidst these uncertainties, with the increase of his family his struggles are greater. He tries to eke out his subsistence by keeping accounts, and writing letters for his neighbours. He strives to be elected parish clerk, or registrar, or clerk to some benefit club. These additions to his income, if he be successful, barely keep him out of debt, and in old age he has no prospect but hopeless indigence and dependence.

To intrust the education of the labouring classes of this country to men involved in such straits, is to condemn the poor to ignorance and its fatal train of evils. To build spacious and well-ventilated schools, without attempting to provide a position of honour and emolument for the masters, is to cheat the poor with a cruel illusion. Even the very small number of masters now well trained in Normal and Model Schools, will find no situation in which their emoluments and prospects will be equal to those which their new acquirements and skill might insure if they should desert the profession of an elementary schoolmaster. Whilst their condition remains without improvement, a religious motive alone can induce the young men, who are now trained in Normal Schools, to sacrifice all prospects of personal advancement for the self-denying and arduous duties of a teacher of the children of the poor. Unless, therefore, concurrently with the arrangements made for training masters of superior acquirements and skill, efforts be also made to provide them with situations of decent comfort, and the prospect of a suitable provision for sickness and old age, they will be driven by necessity, or attracted by superior advantages, to commercial pursuits.

It may be well that the poor should give proof of the value they attach to the education of their children, by making some sacrifice from their earnings to promote the comfort of the schoolmaster, and should thus preserve a consciousness of their right to choose the school in which their children are to be trained, and to exercise some vigilance over the conduct of their master; but the social condition of the poor must be greatly superior to what the most sanguine can expect it will become in the next half-century, before they can afford to provide an adequate subsistence for the schoolmaster; and their moral and intellectual state must be at least equally improved, before they are prepared by the value they attach to the education of their children, to make sacrifices adequate to the remuneration of the teacher.

From the contributions of the poor, therefore, little more can be expected in aid of the master's income, and that increase, if procurable, must be derived both from a more lively appreciation of the benefits of education to a labouring man, and from an improvement in his own means of subsistence.

But if it were otherwise, it may be doubted whether it would be a wise policy to make the schoolmaster dependent on the parents of his scholars for his entire income, for this would be to subject him to the caprices of the least intelligent classes, who would also certainly be the most vigilant and rigorous superiors.

Moreover, a provident charity can, by means of the village school, most gracefully interfere to elevate the condition of the poor, without undermining their independence or teaching them habits of servility; it would not therefore be wise to deprive the rich of a means of expressing their sympathy with the condition of the poor by means of a charity, in which the virtue of self-denial is not obscured by the degradation of the recipient.

The contributions which are annually dependent on the will of the donor, likewise afford him a most effectual means of stimulating the exertions of the master, and thus place the school to a great degree under the influence of the superior classes of society.

On these grounds, while on the one hand it may be doubted whether it is expedient to supersede either the weekly payments of the parents of the scholars, or the contributions of the more wealthy classes, by any fixed sources of income; on the other it is evident, that to leave the master dependent on the poor, and on the fluctuating charity of the rich, is to subject him, in the great majority of cases, to poverty in his office and to indigence and dependence when deprived of it by sickness or old age.

A certain portion of the schoolmaster's income should be attached to his office independently of all local sources of fluctuation and change; he should enjoy his house rent-free, and if possible be provided with a garden and fuel. If then an estimate be made of his salary, on a scale equal to the position he ought to hold in society, one-third of this income should be certain. The smallest sum which ought to be secured to the master, besides a comfortable dwelling, should be £15 or £20, as part of an income of £45 or £60 per annum, and the condition of the master cannot be deemed respectably provided for, unless an income of £30 per annum be secured to him, besides what may be derived from school-pence, and from the contributions of the wealthy, which ought at least to raise this income to £90 per annum.

While the condition of the master is one of such privation and uncertainty, he has by the existing system of school instruction been placed in a situation, the difficulties of which are insuperable, even by the highest talent and skill, much less by men struggling with penury, exhausted with care, often ill-instructed, and sometimes assuming the duties of a most responsible office, only because deemed incompetent to strive for a livelihood in the open field of competition. Men so circumstanced, have been placed, without other assistants than monitors, in charge of schools containing from 150 to 300 scholars and upwards. The monitors usually employed are under twelve years of age, some of them being as young as eight or nine, and they are in general very ignorant, rude, and unskilful. The system of monitorial instruction has practically failed in this country because of the early period at which children are required for manufacturing and agricultural labour. It has been generally abandoned on the Continent on account of its comparative imperfection under any circumstances, but it was probably never exhibited under greater disadvantages than in England.

The earliest efforts of recent promoters of the education of the labouring classes were made in towns. The schools of towns are commonly large—the children are sent to work at a very early age—the population is migratory, and the school attendance short, irregular, and uncertain. One master was placed over a school containing for the most part from 200 to 400 children, and he was not supplied with any assistance, excepting what he could derive from the scholars committed to his charge. His own efforts to create an instructed class, which might render him this service, were constantly thwarted by the migration of the parents, by the removal of the child to work, and the extreme difficulty of combining the instruction and training of the monitorial class with such an attention to the whole school as would preserve order and discipline, and secure so much progress in the several classes as to furnish a proper succession in the first class of ripe scholars from whom to select the monitors.

Under such difficulties few masters succeeded in this country in creating and maintaining efficient monitorial schools, but they have succeeded exactly in proportion as they were enabled by local circumstances to retain the monitors beyond the age of 13 at the school, or were permitted by the trustees to pay them a small weekly stipend for their services, if they also gave them the advantage of separate instruction.

If this be the condition of the master, and if this be the character of the only assistance afforded him in the discipline and instruction of his school, is it a legitimate subject of surprise, that a very large proportion of the children attending elementary schools in this country should not even acquire the art of reading accurately, much less with ease and expression, and that all the higher aims of education should appear, notwithstanding constant school extension, to be unattainable? Can we wonder that the working classes should attach no value to an education so meager and worthless, and consequently that the school attendance of their children should not exceed a year and a half on the average throughout entire districts? Is it surprising that juvenile delinquency should be on the increase?

There are other features connected with the condition of elementary schools which are equally to be deplored. Too commonly their prosperity depends on the exertions

and sacrifices of some benevolent individual. In Church
of England schools, the labour and burthen of their maintenance often depend on the parochial clergyman; in
Dissenting Schools, on some layman, who exhausts his
resources and his time on the task of constantly rebuilding
what always threatens to become a ruin. Even this want
of sympathy of the laity of the Church, and the congregations of Dissenters, in the prosperity of their schools,
is probably, in the first instance, a consequence of that
inefficiency, which their apathy tends to perpetuate. The
school exists, but produces no fruit; no one perceives that
it exercises a civilising influence; when visited it is a
scene of noise and disorder. It is obvious to a toil-worn
member of the middle class of this country, that he has
neither leisure, nor superfluous energy, to undertake the
task of introducing order into this Babel. It fails to interest his sympathies; consequently elementary schools are
visited by their supporters chiefly on the annual field-day
of a paraded exhibition, when the children are initiated
in a public imposture, and the promoters of the school
are the willing and conscious dupes of a pious fraud.

The influence which the inadequacy of voluntary contributions, for the support of a system of elementary education, exerts on the condition even of the most prosperous
Normal Schools, is not less remarkable.

The Normal Schools are at present supported partly by
funds contributed by the Central Societies and Diocesan
Boards, and partly by the sums paid by the patrons or
friends of students to procure their settlement in the profession of schoolmasters, by obtaining for them the benefit
of training in a Normal School.

As the Central Society contributes for the most part
only half the requisite funds, or even less, the selection
of the candidates for admission is narrowed to the class

who are able and willing to pay for the admission of their children and dependents, and to the individuals whom they may present as candidates.

Unfortunately the tendency is to select young men wanting those natural energies, physical or mental, requisite for success in an independent career in life, and to seek, by means of the Normal Schools, to introduce into the profession of schoolmaster young persons, not from any peculiar fitness for this vocation, but rather on account of the absence of qualifications for any other.

The Principals of Normal Schools therefore complain, not only of their want of preparation for the course of instruction given in the Training Schools, because the candidates have not been grounded in ordinary elementary knowledge, but of the absence of the proper physical, mental, and moral qualifications. It is reported that a great number of the candidates and students of the Normal Schools show signs of scrofula, and that generally their physical temperament is sluggish and inert. They have too often had no further instruction than what can be obtained in an elementary school of average character, during the usual period of attendance, till 13 years of age. They do not for the most part enter into the profession from inclination, and it is therefore proportionately difficult to give the right moral direction to their minds, and to kindle in them energies equal to the difficulties they must encounter.

Ill-adapted as this class of students is for success in the Normal School, and likely as they are to fail in the elementary school when their training is (with whatever care) completed, the number of candidates presented by patrons and friends, on the terms of payment required by the Normal Schools, is barely sufficient to keep these schools in activity. There is therefore no opportunity for selection; and unless other sources be developed, even this imperfect supply is precarious, and liable soon to fail.

On these grounds it is of the utmost importance to the future prosperity of the Normal Schools, that the elementary schools should be rendered the means of educating a class of candidates for admission, who in their earliest youth should have been selected on account of their proficiency and skill, and whose progress in the several grades of monitor, pupil teacher, and assistant teacher, should not only have been the object of systematic care and continual vigilance, but whose ultimate selection should be made by the Inspector on the ground of their superiority, as proved by the experience of years, in all the qualifications required for success in the vocation of a schoolmaster.

On the other hand, it is important to provide for the Normal Schools a means of support which shall guarantee their efficiency by ensuring the application of the money to the completion of the training of teachers, whose instruction, character, and skill, have been the objects of years of vigilance and care.

The Minutes of the Committee of Council on Education in August and December 1846, were intended to provide remedies for the evils which have been described in this chapter. Their Lordships desired to render the profession of schoolmaster honourable, by raising its character, by giving it the public recognition of impartially awarded certificates or diplomas, and by securing to well-trained or otherwise efficient masters a position of comfort during the period of their arduous labours, and the means of retirement on a pension awarded by the Government. They were also anxious to lighten their ill-requited toil in the school, by providing them with the aid of assistant teachers trained and instructed under their own eye, and adequate in number to the efficient management of the school.

The arrangements for rearing a body of skilful and highly instructed masters are to commence in the school itself, by the selection of the most deserving and proficient of the scholars, who are to be apprenticed from the age of 13 to that of 18. By the regulations determining the character of this apprenticeship, the school is to be in a condition fitting it to become a sphere for the training of a candidate for the office of schoolmaster. A great stimulus is thus offered to the scholars to qualify themselves by good conduct and by their attainments, for appointment as pupil teachers; to the promoters of the school to render its condition complete as respects fittings, apparatus, and the supply of books; and to the schoolmaster, so to order the discipline and instruction of the school, as to raise it to the proper standard of efficiency. But no requirements are made, limiting the discretion of the trustees, in the selection or dismissal of the master or mistress, in the dismissal of any assistant or pupil teacher, or either as to the books and apparatus to be used, the system of organisation to be adopted, or the methods of instruction to be pursued.

In each year of the apprenticeship, the pupil teacher is to be examined by Her Majesty's Inspector in a course of instruction, the subjects of which are enumerated in the regulations. Great care is to be taken that he lives in a household where he will be under the constant influence of a good example. His religious instruction is to be conducted by the master of the school. In Church of England schools, this religious instruction will for the most part be under the superintendence of the parochial clergyman, but whenever the managers of the school are disposed to permit the apprenticeship in a Church of England school of a scholar whose parents do not belong to the Church of England, their Lordships have no desire to fetter their discretion in that respect, and would acquiesce in any reasonable arrangements which might be made between the managers and the parents for the religious training of their children. Though their Lordships have not by any of their Minutes attempted to enforce, they are nevertheless desirous to promote by their sanction and encouragement, such arrangements in Church of England schools as may provide for the admission of the children of persons not members of the Church of England, without any requirements inconsistent with the rights of conscience.

In schools not connected with the Church of England, the Committee of Council, acting on the third regulation of the 24th September, 1839, and on the Minute specially communicated to the British and Foreign School Society as related in the last chapter, will not direct the Inspector of such schools to examine the religious instruction of the apprentice. They desire to enable the promoters of schools connected with dissenting congregations, to accept the advantages impartially offered by their Minutes, without entering into any compromise of the opinions they entertain as to religious endowments. On these grounds their Lordships declare that they will accept the certificate of the managers of such schools that they are satisfied with the state of the religious knowledge of the pupil teacher. The Committee of Council thus intend to avoid making any requirement as to the character of such religious teaching beyond that contained in their Minute of the 3rd of December, 1839 (quoted in the last chapter), which states that 'the daily reading of a portion of the Scriptures shall form part of the instruction' of the school; nor do their Lordships require attendance on any particular Sunday school, or on any particular place of public worship; but at the close of each year will be satisfied if the managers certify that the pupil teachers have been attentive to their religious duties.

The scholars selected for apprenticeship will for the most part belong to families supported by manual labour; there is thus open to the children of such families, a career which could otherwise be rarely commenced. The first steps of their entrance into the honourable profession of a schoolmaster will be attended with an alleviation of the burthens, often ill-sustained by their parents, of supporting a family by manual industry. The pupil teacher will receive directly from the Government a stipend increasing from £10 at the close of the first year to £20 at the close of the fifth year of his apprenticeship. In many cases it is probable that the good conduct of the apprentice will secure additional rewards from the managers of the school, such as a supply of text-books on the prescribed subjects of instruction, or an annual grant of clothes, or an addition to his stipend. At the close of the apprenticeship, every pupil teacher who has passed the annual examination will be entitled to a certificate, declaring that he has successfully completed his apprenticeship. This certificate, as a testimonial of character and of attainments, would be in itself an invaluable introduction to the confidence of a merchant, or of the member of a learned profession, if the apprentice should then determine not to pursue the vocation of a schoolmaster. But the Government have extended their provident care even further. Every pupil teacher provided with a certificate at the close of his apprenticeship, may become a candidate for one or two employments under the patronage of the Government. In each Inspector's district, an annual examination will be held, to which all apprentices who have obtained their certificates will be admitted, to compete for the distinction of an exhibition entitling them to be sent as Queen's scholars to a Normal School under their Lordships' inspection. Such pupil teachers as are successful in obtaining a Queen's Scholarship, will thus be enabled to complete their training as schoolmasters, by passing through the course of discipline and instruction provided in a Normal School. They will thus have an opportunity of increasing their knowledge, improving their acquaintance with the best methods of instruction, and of becoming more experienced in the organisation and discipline of schools. At the close of each year's instruction in the Normal School, the students will be examined by one or more of Her Majesty's Inspectors, and upon such examination, their Lordships will award a certificate denoting one of three degrees of merit. Every master who leaves the Normal School with a certificate of the first degree of merit will be entitled to a grant of £15 or £20 per annum. If he obtain a certificate of the second degree of merit, a grant of £20 or £25 per annum; and for a certificate of the third degree of merit a grant of £25 or £30 per annum, on condition that the trustees and managers of the school of which he may have charge provide him with a house rent-free, and with a further salary equal to twice the amount of the grant.

A poor man's child may thus, at the age of thirteen, not only cease to be a burthen to his father's family, but enter a profession at every step in which his mind will expand, and his intellect be stored, and, with the blessing of God, his moral and religious character developed. His success will be acknowledged by certificates from authority. Honorary distinctions connected with solid advantages will be open to him. He may attain a position the lowest rewards of which are, that he shall occupy a comfortable dwelling, rent-free, with a salary of £45 or £60 per annum; and which may, if he complete his course of training be raised to a minimum stipend of £90 per annum.

Instead of having before him a life of arduous, ill-requited, and necessarily unsuccessful toil, if he had otherwise entered the profession of a schoolmaster, he will, on his settlement as master of a school, be enabled to organise that school with apprenticed assistants conducted by himself through a prescribed course of instruction from the age of 13 to that of 18. Thus aided by apprentices selected on account of merit, whose education will be completed under the eye of a vigilant inspection, his school will reward him by becoming a scene of order, and his scholars by their cheerful obedience and success. It will be the duty of the master to instruct the apprentices daily during one hour and a half after the usual school time, and to teach them the management of a school. If the numbers under his charge amount to 150, he may have six apprentices, and he will then receive a further addition of £21 per annum to his salary as a remuneration for the time and care bestowed on the education of these apprentices. A school so conducted could not fail to attract the confidence of the neighbouring poor. They would soon discover the great practical advantages of its discipline in moulding the habits, increasing the knowledge, and developing the mental energies of their children. They would perceive that education was not an unreal abstraction, affording no practical advantage, but a powerful means of promoting success in life, and of securing the happiness of their children.

On the other hand, if, at the close of his apprenticeship, the pupil-teacher shall be unable at the public competition to procure a Queen's Scholarship, the Government have opened to the unsuccessful candidates appointments in departments of the public service, which have hitherto been the objects of purely political patronage. The parents of poor families in the neighbourhood of any school will have an obvious interest in its efficiency, as a means of procuring for their children admission into departments of the public service with double or treble the wages of a working man, and the prospect of further promotion.

The Committee of Council have also shown a just consideration for the interest of the masters who, not having received a regular training in a Normal School, have at present charge of elementary education. Notwithstanding the low standard of acquirements, and the want of skill generally prevalent among the existing race of schoolmasters, there are among them men whose natural energies have triumphed over the difficulties of a neglected and ill-paid profession, and who, by self-education and natural sagacity, have attained a just reputation. The Committee of Council, desirous to avoid a practical injustice to such masters, and to offer incentives to all other teachers who may now have charge of schools, to qualify themselves for certificates, have resolved to admit untrained masters to an examination for three classes of certificates, corresponding with those to be granted in Normal Schools. The augmentation of salary annexed to such certificates will therefore be accessible to all meritorious schoolmasters; and, as it will not be necessary that a man of good education should, in order to enjoy this advantage, pass through the course of instruction given in a Normal School, the profession will probably attract men of character and acquirements.

The honour and emoluments of any profession are obviously among the chief inducements to its adoption. For the first time in the career of schoolmasters, they may obtain from authority the certificate of a successfully completed apprenticeship—the rank of Queen's Scholar, and three diplomas, denoting three degrees of attainments and merit. Through the whole period of their education, the Government offers rewards to stimulate exertions, and at length assists to establish them in a condition of comfort and respectability. These are circumstances likely in themselves to induce masters of schools to remain in their profession, even if we can suppose them to be insensible to motives of a higher character. But it is impossible to secure any position against vicissitude, and especially to prevent a deserving man from being plunged into privation by disabling sickness or infirmity, or robbed by unavoidable calamity of a provision for old age. Their Lordships have, therefore, rendered superannuation pensions accessible to masters distinguished by long and efficient services (adopting, as a minimum period, fifteen years, seven of which must have been spent in a school subject to inspection), and who by age or by any disabling infirmity are compelled to retire. It cannot be doubted that such arrangements will raise this profession in public estimation, by increasing its efficiency and respectability.

The Normal School is the most important institution in a system of elementary education. It has been before shown how desirable it is that the Normal School should be fed with students from the *élite* of the scholars educated in elementary schools. It cannot be expected that members of the middle class of society will, to any great extent in this country, choose the vocation of teachers of the poor. The system which renders Normal Schools dependent on that ambiguous support, rather intended to befriend persons of feeble character or physically infirm, than to give the largest amount of efficiency to elementary instruction, must impair the results which might otherwise be attained. To make every elementary school a scene of exertion, from which the highest ranks of teachers may be entered by the humblest scholar, is to render the profession of schoolmasters popular among the poor, and to offer to their children the most powerful incentives to learning. Every boy of character and ability who is first among his fellows may select this career, and in the majority of cases will do so. In his whole course he will be in vigorous competition with the pupil teachers of other schools; and thus the Queen's Scholars, who, after a public trial, are selected for admission into the Normal Schools, will be naturally the most gifted, and by persevering application, the best instructed and most skilful youths, which the elementary schools of the country can rear. Instead, therefore, of the complaint which the Principals of Normal Schools now make, that the students entering them are deficient in physical and mental energy, and for the most part in knowledge even of the humblest rudiments of learning; the Queen's Scholars who are after public competition admitted, will have passed through an elementary course of instruction in religion, in English grammar and composition, in the history of their country, in arithmetic, algebra, mensuration, the rudiments of mechanics, in the art of land-surveying and levelling, in geography, and such elements of nautical astronomy as are comprised in the use of the globes. Their skill in conducting a class will have been developed by five years' experience as assistants in a common school. To these attainments will in many cases be added a knowledge of the theory and skill in the art of vocal music, and also, in some cases, of drawing from models, or linear drawing. The Normal Schools, therefore, will be fed with a class of students much superior to that which now enters them.

The expense of supporting a Normal School in efficiency is a burthen too heavy to be borne by purely voluntary contributions. The cost of the maintenance and education of each student is about £50 per annum; the annual expenditure on a Normal School, containing 100 students, must therefore be £5000. If the training of each student be continued for three years, little more than 30 schoolmasters will annually enter the profession from such a school, and when the number of schools which ought to exist in the country is compared with this annual supply, it is obvious that if Normal Schools are to be the chief sources from which the ranks of this profession are to be replenished, the outlay for the support of such a system is in itself greater than anything which has ever been contemplated by a scheme of purely charitable contribution. Their Lordships have, however, by the plan of apprenticeship, at the same time provided both for the increased efficiency of the elementary school, and for the completion of a considerable portion of the training of the candidate before he enters the Normal School; it is probable, therefore, that the period of instruction in Normal Schools may in the case of Queen's Scholars be reduced from three years to a shorter term. The remaining expenses are in part to be met by assistance afforded by the Government. Every Queen's Scholar will have an exhibition of £20 or £25, which sum will be applied towards the expenses attending his education during the first year in a Normal School. At the close of that year, if he be successful in obtaining a certificate, a second contribution of £20 will be made to the school, so that in the first year of the training of a Queen's Scholar, four-fifths of the expense may be borne by the Government. At the close of the second year £25 are to be paid, and at the close of the third year £30, if the student obtain a certificate of merit in each year. In the two latter years, therefore, the Government will defray one-half of the cost of his training. With such liberal arrangements for their support, it is probable that the number of Normal Schools will rapidly increase. A wide scope is still left for charitable contributions towards the erection of the requisite buildings, two-thirds of which outlay must be derived from private subscriptions; and in the maintenance of the schools, one-third at least of the expense will devolve on private charity, even if the Queen's Scholars should form a considerable proportion of the students entering the schools. One-half the charge of educating candidates who are not Queen's Scholars, will obviously devolve on private benevolence.

The efficiency of elementary schools will doubtless establish the confidence of the poor in these institutions, and increase the period of school attendance for their children. Some time must however elapse, ere parents struggling with poverty will consent to forego even those small additions to the weekly income of their families, which are derived from the humble earnings of their children at a tender age. The difference of popular opinion in Scotland on the advantage of education for the child of a poor man, as compared with that sentiment in England, is a remarkable proof of the natural influence of a system of national education, in raising the estimate among the poor of the value of mental and moral endowments. In Scotland, especially among the rural population, every labourer is willing to undergo privations to provide that education for his children which he deems essential to their success in this life, and to their preparation for another state of existence. This opinion is grounded not more on a shrewd estimate of the causes which promote the advancement of their children, than of that deep religious instinct which characterises the Scotch as a nation. There is nothing in the opinion of the poor in England as to the value of education, at all comparable to the sagacious foresight and profound and pious feeling which prompt the Scotch parent to make sacrifices for this object. The Committee of Council have however been unwilling, in the absence of such sentiments, to resort to any compulsory arrangements to procure school attendance. Such expedients they have regarded as ill suited to the genius of this country; they have been desirous to vindicate the parental right to determine the nature and extent of the education to be given to the child, and to promote the growth of a livelier sense of the benefits of education by the increased efficiency of the schools, and also by arrangements intended to show the labouring man, that considerable knowledge and mental cultivation are compatible with the hardihood necessary to sustain the rudest forms of toil, and to meet the privations of a labourer's life. With this view their Lordships have been disposed to promote the establishment of Schools of Industry. In rural districts, field-gardens may be advantageously connected with the school. The master may superintend the instruction of the scholars during half the day in the culture of a garden, and may devote the rest of the time to the ordinary school instruction. If the school field-garden were divided into allotments, for which a rent was paid by the scholars, the cultivation of these garden plots would afford a larger addition to the income of the labourer's family, than the earnings of a child in the casual employments of farming labour.

In the denser parts of great cities, a large, and possibly an increasing number of children have no training in any handicraft, but seek a precarious livelihood by costermongering; by casual employment in errands; and in small services to persons whom they encounter in the streets. Such habits naturally tend to mendicancy, vagrancy, petty thefts, and the criminal career and vagabond life of a juvenile delinquent. Such children have often no home; the father is dead, or has absconded; the mother may be a prostitute, or may have married and deserted her offspring; or the child has fled from the drunken violence or loathsome selfishness of his parents. Many sleep under the open arches of the markets, or of the areas of the houses of ancient construction; in deserted buildings, out-houses, and cellars, and rise in the morning not knowing where or how to obtain a meal. Others are driven forth by their parents to beg or to steal, and not allowed to eat until they have brought home the produce of their knavery or cunning. Some live in the haunts of professed thieves, are trained in all the arts of pilfering, instructed how to elude the police, and to evade the law. They are reared to regard society as their enemy, and property as a monstrous institution on which they may justly prey. The majority of this class of children are practically heathens. They probably never heard the name of Christ. Christianity has done nothing for them.

The most obvious advantage to be offered to such children is the means of earning a livelihood by training them in some handicraft requiring skill. If every such child had the opportunity of entering a workshop in which he could acquire the art of a smith, or a carpenter, or a cooper, or other similar trade, and after some hours of application was provided with a coarse but wholesome meal, it is not to be doubted that many, attracted not less by the sympathy which such arrangements would prove to exist for their forlorn condition, than by the opportunity of escaping from the misery of a life of crime and privation, would become assiduous scholars in such schools of industry. If also an hour or two daily were set apart for instruction in the general outline of Christian faith and duty, and in the rudiments of humble learning, how many children might we not hope would be saved from ruin. To promote such arrangements, their Lordships have offered assistance towards the erection of the requisite buildings, towards the purchase of tools, and for the encouragement of the master workmen by granting gratuities for every boy who, in consequence of skill acquired in the workshop, shall have become a workman or assistant in any trade or craft whereby he is earning a livelihood.

The domestic arrangements of the poor are often extremely defective, from the want of a knowledge of the commonest arts and maxims of household economy. A girl who works in a factory or a mine, or who is employed from an early hour in the morning until the evening in field labour, has little or no opportunity to acquire the habits and skill of a housewife. Even the rudest traditions of domestic thrift are liable to be lost, when public employment interferes so much with the proper training of the labourer's daughter at home. Commerce offers a larger variety of productions for the sustenance of the common people of this country, than of any other; but they are unacquainted with the use of any articles of food besides those which are of home production, with the exception of tea, coffee, and sugar. From these defects, a considerable portion of the earnings of the labourer is unskilfully wasted, his home is deprived of comfort which he might otherwise enjoy, and discontent often drives him to dissipation.

To remedy these evils it has been proposed to make the school itself a means of instructing and training girls in the arts of domestic economy. It has been conceived, that a considerable portion of the oral lessons given in the girls' school, might be devoted to the subject of household management, and that if a wash-house and kitchen were connected with the school, they might, by proper arrangements, receive a practical training in cottage cookery, and in the care of the clothes of a labourer's family. For the encouragement of such plans their Lordships have proposed to grant assistance towards the erection of the requisite buildings, and gratuities to the mistress for success in the instruction of her scholars.

The social tendencies of the plans contemplated in the Minutes of the Committee of Council on Education for August and December, 1846, are, therefore, to raise the character and position of the schoolmaster; to provide for him a respectable competency; to make arrangements for rearing a race of more highly instructed masters by the establishment and support of a larger number of Normal Schools; to feed those Normal Schools with candidates having much higher attainments and greater skill and energy than those which have hitherto entered them; to render the school popular among the poor, as a means of introducing their children to more honourable and profitable employments, and by its increased efficiency to create in the minds of the working class a juster estimate of the value of education for their children. These combined influences will, it is hoped, raise considerably the standard of instruction among the humbler classes, and promote the growth of a truly Christian civilisation.

SOURCE: *Four Periods*, pp. 451–456, 471–493. The original title of the pamphlet was *The School in Its Relations to the State, the Church, and the Congregation.*

6

Letter to Earl Granville, K.G., on the Revised Code of Regulations Contained in the Minutes of the Committee of Council on Education Dated July 29th, 1861
(November 4, 1861)

Faced with the challenge of the Revised Code, Kay-Shuttleworth emerged from retirement to denounce the Code and defend the 1846 Minutes. He took the opportunity to reaffirm his educational philosophy in its most positive and hopeful form. In reply to Robert Lowe's call for more "free trade" in education, he criticizes the misapplication of the principles of political economy. Confronted with Lowe's proposal to concentrate on the three R's, he argues that the nation cannot afford to treat the mass of the people as beasts of burden, but must take steps to develop their intelligence and morality. He derides the sort of rote learning that would inevitably be encouraged by the system of "payment by results"; he defends the higher social and economic status for teachers which he tried to establish in the 1846 Minutes.

Kay-Shuttleworth's letter is addressed to the Lord Presi-

dent of the Privy Council. Robert Lowe was Vice-President of the Privy Council in charge of its Committee on Education.

. . . I trust your Lordship will permit me to submit to the Committee of Council the reasons why the promoters of schools are of opinion that this Revised Code is impracticable, without pulverising the existing system and destroying the connection of the Government with elementary education.

The vindication of the Revised Code is based on the denial that the existing system secures adequate results. By implication it attributes this alleged failure to a misdirection of effort. The teachers are too highly instructed, —they are above their work,—their daily instruction as apprentices and their residence in college must be shortened,—their education must be lowered to the level of their work,—that level is the teaching of reading, writing, and arithmetic, to scholars early absorbed by labour in agriculture or manufactures. This work ought to be done before eleven. No working man's child need be paid for after that age. The teachers have been mischievously pampered and protected: 'Hitherto,' says the Vice-President, 'we have been living under a system of bounties and protection; now we prefer to have a little free trade.' The teachers must, like corn and cotton, be subject to the law of supply and demand. They and the managers must make the best bargains they can. The school managers must be paid only for work done. It is quite easy to test the work their teachers do, by examining every scholar in those elements which alone are the care of the State. If a fair proportion of the scholars learn to read, write, and cypher before they are eleven years old, nothing else is wanted. But to accomplish this—whatever has been the age at

which a child first entered school—whatever his home
training, capacity, or the comparative regularity of his
school attendance,—any school which takes charge of him
must either do so without State aid, or must by some art
lift him up to a fixed standard of attainment, to be required between the ages, respectively, of 3 and 7,—7 and
9,—9 and 11, and 11 upwards. If he knows more and can
do more than is required at his age by this standard, he
must be examined among those who are less proficient
than himself.

The remedy devised in the Code for the defects of the
existing system may be thus defined:—

The most certain way in which to secure the only results
which are the legitimate concern of the State in elementary schools, is to examine each scholar in reading, writing, and arithmetic, and pay the managers a certain sum
per head for each school attendance of every scholar who
can pass an examination in each of these three elements,
according to a standard of attainment to be required at
fixed periods of age, and other conditions set forth in the
Code. . . .

The duties of the Inspector under the Revised Code
would have been most harassing to himself, and would
have occasioned an amount of irritation and controversy
between school-managers and the Education Department
which cannot have been foreseen.

The unavoidable reduction in very many schools would
have amounted to half the annual grants, in some to
much more, and the average deduction would have been
two-fifths.

The Inspector would have been the ostensible instrument of this reduction. He has hitherto exercised greater
influence on the improvement of the schools by his experience and conciliation of co-operative efforts, than by

his power to recommend the withdrawal of the grants to the teachers and pupil teachers for neglect and consequent unsatisfactory results, either in organisation, instruction, or discipline. His time, under the Revised Code, would be consumed in a mechanical drudgery which would necessarily withdraw his attention from the religious and general instruction, and from the moral features of the school. The organisation of the school could not be inspected, for it would be necessarily broken up into groups of age for the purposes of the examination. Scholars with attainments above the Code standard would be degraded to their groups of age, to be placed along with untaught savages, dullards, sluggards, and truants, unable to reach the standard. The managers and teachers would watch anxiously the trial of each child, which was to determine whether twenty-five shillings or nothing was to be awarded to the school.

The scholars of elementary schools are often much disturbed during an inspection, because the examiner is a stranger. He speaks, perhaps, in the most encouraging way, but in a tone of voice, with words and a manner, to which they are not accustomed. The very refinement, gentleness, and scholastic accuracy of the Inspector often puts them out. I have seen scholars examined one day by the curate in some part of one of the Gospels, and reply successfully to questions uttered by one with whose person, manner, voice, words, and method they were quite familiar; and lamentably fail the next day, when questioned with perfect fairness by the Inspector, who was a stranger.

But all Inspectors are not perfect either in manner, utterance, choice of words for poor children, method of examining them; nor in the skill, kindness, and patience required to bring out the true state of the child's knowledge.

This applies forcibly to such elements as reading, writing, and arithmetic, even if the examination is restricted (as apparently intended in the Revised Code) to the most mechanical results, without any examination in the meaning or grammar of what is read, or in that 'logic of the poor'—arithmetic.

If an Inspector enter a school with an abrupt manner and a harsh voice,—if he roughly interfere with the organisation,—scold one or two scholars,—or be hurried, for lack of time or patience,—he will never discover what the children know or can do in their school-work. They will be bewildered. He will get few juniors to read without strange hesitation and mistakes. Few will write correctly 1,000,003 from dictation. Very few will write with their usual skill. A large portion will fail in arithmetical trials, which they would have passed with ease if the clergyman or the master had examined them. Thus the true state of the school is often not known to the Inspector. Experienced Inspectors make allowance for these hindrances in their estimate of the state of the schools under the present form of inspection. That would not, however, be possible if an Inspector had to deal with purely mechanical results, as in the examination in the Revised Code.

But when the results of the Inspector's examination differed widely from that made during the preceding week by the clergyman and teacher, his function would be regarded as the instrument for disallowing the just claims of schools. It would soon become the most unpopular and irksome function in Great Britain. The Privy Council Office would be worried with numerous and reiterated remonstrances. . . .

The teachers settled in elementary schools . . . did not expect that the arbitrary and indefensible application of a doctrine of political economy respecting supply and demand, bounties and protection, to a sphere of action in which it has never had any place in English statesmanship —to a sphere of moral action in which it is totally inapplicable—would cause an abrupt and total change in every element of their position.

Similar errors in the application of doctrines of pure economy to questions in which moral elements greatly predominate have been committed before. Thus, because, at the time of the reformation of the relief of indigence, the children of independent labourers were either without schools, or in very bad schools, it was said that the pauper children in workhouses ought not to be well instructed, lest their better education should operate as an encouragement to pauperism. The fallacy here consisted not simply in a neglect of the consideration that education is the most efficient antidote to hereditary pauperism; but still more in a cynical and sceptical denial of all moral obligation on the part of the State to these children.

In like manner, the protection of women, and of children under 13, from excessive labour in manufactories and mines, has been resisted as a violation of the principles of free trade. Trade, it is said, should be free from all State regulation. If this were so, trade might exist in slaves—or workmen might be reduced to the condition of serfs or slaves—or the physical and moral condition of the people might be subject to any degree of degradation, while the interference of the Government for the interests of the commonwealth would be shut out by an inexorable abstract principle of political economy.

The fallacy in the application of the principles of free trade to the education of the people resembles these. The Parliament and the Executive Government are the guardians of our mixed constitution,—they represent the nation,—but they are collectively a power created by the people for the promotion and conservation of national interests. This central power is embodied in the word State. The central authority has a greater interest, collectively, in the intelligence and virtue of the people than any fragment of the nation can have. On that intelligence and virtue depend respect for the law,—the right discharge of civil functions and political franchises,—the due subordination to authority—the harmony of classes,—the development of the natural resources of the country and its power,—the increase of commerce, wealth, comfort, and national contentment,—the public spirit of citizens,—the valour of armies and navies,—and the national patriotism in sustaining the constitution alike against invasion and against internal corruption or revolution. But the education of the mass is not a want to be so felt, when ignorance and coarse habits prevail among them, as to create a supply by the act of the uneducated classes. Education infiltrates from the upper and governing classes to the lower. All civilisation is primarily the work of inventive genius. The lesson such minds have to teach is first imparted to the upper and governing classes. Its benefits descend from them to the lower. These uncivilised classes are trained by example and discipline; they are, as minors are, the care of the governing classes in some form,—they do not seek to be civilised and taught, as an original and irrepressible want, but they are sought by the missionary, by the teacher, by the agent of industrial progress, and they are rescued, not by their own act, but by that of the State and the upper classes, to whom their progress has become a social and political necessity. But the State—that is, the most able governing minds in the counsels of the sovereign

power—is more likely to perceive this want of the commonwealth than even the middle classes; for the collec-
tive dangers from national ignorance and barbarism are
greater, and the cost of national pauperism, crime, and
disorder, are more apparent to the Government than they
can be to individuals. Consequently, the education of the
people has, throughout Europe, and in this country, originated in a great degree with the State. But if we were to
suppose that education received no aid from the central
authority, or the national resources from taxation, it
would still be an error to speak of free trade in education.
The several education societies certainly have a friendly
rivalry in their efforts to found and support schools, and
to attract children to them. The State in no way interferes
with their freedom in doing this; but it is not trade. This
work is not done for pecuniary profit; it is done under
the influence of a sense of moral and religious obligation,
and a conviction that the wealth and strength of States,
and domestic peace and prosperity, depend on the moral
and intellectual elevation of the people. There is the
utmost amount of civil and religious liberty for such
efforts; there is no lack of freedom in such work, which
however is not trade. To pretend that it is trade—and on
that pretence to invoke the application of an abstract
principle to shut out the aid of the State—is by a fallacy
to attempt to limit the power of the State to promote the
intelligence and virtue of the people, in which it has a
larger stake than any fragment of the people, even than
the Church established by law.

It is impossible, then, to justify any part of the Revised
Code by an appeal to the principles of free trade. The
teachers of elementary schools have not, under the Minutes of 1846, been so much the subjects of 'protection and

bounties' as the masters of the endowed schools of Edward the Sixth and Elizabeth, or the masters or presidents and fellows of colleges, and the professors of universities. . . .

The Government is responsible for the present character of schools, in all their details. It invented the pupil-teacher apprenticeship, and the Training Colleges. It convinced the religious communions, by the earnest advocacy of its own authorised agents, that the education of the poor ought to be raised to its present standard. It has vigilantly superintended the execution of its Minutes by its own Inspectors. At any moment it might have required more drill in elementary subjects by schoolmasters. One circular letter would have ensured the closest attention to the subject. It even neglected to carry into execution the last clause of the Minute of the 2nd of April, 1853, devised for this express purpose, in schools which might obtain that capitation grant. The whole curriculum of study has been regulated by its examinations of the Training Colleges, of certificated teachers, and of pupil teachers. This curriculum might have been modified at any time. The Government is therefore identified with what exists. The present level of popular instruction has been the result of its administration. The work is confessedly incomplete, but for its condition in this stage of progress, the Committee of Council is primarily, in all respects, responsible. It has, however, contributed only one-third of the cost. The £4,800,000 expended by the Government, have been met by double that sum raised locally. The total outlay in building, enlarging, and improving 27 Training Colleges has been £334,981, of which £101,641 were derived from the Government, and £223,339 from other sources. Yet the State, as the contributor of only one-third, arrogates to itself the right to say that all that is done is wrong,

though the Education Societies, the Diocesan and Archi-
diaconal Boards of Education, the committees and Principals of Training Colleges, cling to the principles of the
existing system, and to the great majority of its details.
Especially, when the State has thus invented and stimulated a system which has cost its promoters £9,600,000, by
an outlay of one-half of that amount of public money, it
has incurred obligations to those who have expended
nearly ten millions, in the confidence that the Executive
was not a mere abstraction, but a power capable of con-
tracting moral obligations. The character of a system of
public education thus created, ought not to be abruptly
and harshly changed by the fiat of a Minister, without the
consent of the great controlling bodies and communions
who have expended twice as much as the State. Even were
Parliament to make such a change, it would be a national
dishonour. It would be an act of repudiation ever to be
remembered with shame.

But not only would such an abrupt change be disgraceful, it would be short-sighted statesmanship; it would be
a present saving, with the certainty of an ultimate disastrous loss. Otherwise, all those who have depended on the
growth of Christian civilisation for the diminution of
pauperism and crime have been dreamers. The protection
of the public peace from tumult—of private property from
depredation,—the detection, pursuit, trial, and punishment of crime,—cost the nation £9,000,000 annually, without taking into account the loss of wealth by robbers,
incendiaries, and rioters. Pauperism, which is the hereditary consequence of generations of ignorance, superstition, and the slow and partial emancipation of the people
from a previous state of serfdom, costs £6,000,000 annually. This relief of indigence is simply a measure of police.
The life of the indigent is protected, as at the very founda-

tion of laws for the protection of property and the public peace. The alternative would be a vast increase of vaga-bondage, crime, and tumult.

But this system of police for the restraint of crime and pauperism, has little or nothing in it that tends to cure those disorders. All curative agencies are of a totally dif-ferent character. They are purely moral agencies. Their operation is gradual; it is felt only in a generation of men, or in successive generations. Such agencies appeal to the faith of great Statesmen, who are alone capable of guid-ing nations. A Statesman who foresees the necessity of providing for a great though remote danger, threatening the independence of his country, trains the population to arms; inspires them with a martial spirit; year by year strengthens citadels and erects batteries on the coasts; ac-cumulates the munitions of war; and creates a great navy. The arsenals and dockyards, the citadels and forts, after years of preparation, contain a vast accumulation of the means of national defence. The nation, too, is armed, disciplined, and filled with a patriotic spirit. That con-ception of the necessity of thus meeting a great emergency is the result of the experience which history records. In like manner, a confidence in the efficacy of moral agencies in the diminution of crime and pauperism, results from a careful study of the history of the emancipation of the humblest classes of any European nation from serfdom, helotry, and villenage. The primary agent in this has been Christianity, which has taught the moral equality of all men in the eye of God. This idea, notwithstanding inferi-orities of race, renders the slavery of accountable human beings ultimately impossible in Christian nations. It is equally impossible that responsible moral agents should be allowed to be the victims of mere animal instinct, of ignorance, of the want of moral, religious, and mental culture, in any Christian people. Crime and pauperism are—in the degree in which they now exist—the heir-looms of the state of serfdom. They are the signs of the partial nature of the emancipation of the people from a brutish condition in which they were used like more intelligent beasts of burthen. But that Statesman who refuses to make an immediate outlay on the religious education of the people, in order to humanise their manners, correct their habits, increase their intelligence, and raise their moral condition, or prefers to cripple such an outlay for the sake of some immediate paltry economy, is not only short-sighted, but he must in his heart disbelieve the efficacy of moral and religious agencies as antidotes to pauperism and crime.

The force of the confidence in these agencies which exists in the nation, may be measured by the fact that the Education Grant is the only part of the fund derived from national taxation which, by its expenditure, now produces a voluntary contribution twice as great, and which by a gradual change, extending over fifteen years, may be made to produce from local sources, contributions thrice as large, as the public grant. Would a Chancellor of the Exchequer be farsighted who should put this result in peril, if not render it impossible, by an abrupt and harsh change?

Recently proposals have been submitted to successive Parliaments for a reduction of the county franchise to a rating occupation of £10, and of the borough franchise to one of £6. Nothing tended to defeat these measures so much as the alarm excited in the middle classes by the proceedings of the Trades' Unions. These combinations often attempted to regulate labour so as to interfere with the freedom of workmen, and dictated to capital so as to usurp the authority necessary to successful enterprise.

The domination of the Unions was generally without the violence and vindictiveness of former times. But it was arbitrary—was often directed to objects so mischievous or impracticable, as to inspire a deep-seated aversion to the extension of the franchise by the reduction of the property qualification. That proposal for including a larger number of the most intelligent and morally deserving portion of the working classes within the pale of the constitution is indefinitely postponed. But all parties agreed in the importance of devising the means of sifting out the best representatives of the classes supported by manual labour from the mass, and conferring the franchise on them. The effect of a steady perseverance in a system of national education, such as is at present in operation, would be to raise such men within the pale of the constitution. The 23,000 teachers and pupil teachers will certainly all possess the franchise. They are nearly all children of parents supported by manual labour, or of persons not possessing the franchise. Their elevation is a type of the true and certain influence of the same kind of training on the mass. The fifty-eight millions annually expended on beer, spirits, and tobacco will be reduced. The money thus saved will be devoted to the rent of more comfortable houses, to better household management, to the education of the children. A better-housed population will soon have many heads of families within the pale of the present franchise.

To give the people a worse education from motives of short-sighted economy, would be, in these respects, utterly inconsistent with all preceding national policy. The idea that an ignorant, brutish people is either more subordinate or more easily controlled than a people loyal by conviction and contented from experience and reason, is exploded. The notion that the mass of the people are the sources of national wealth merely as beasts of burthen— that the nation has no interest in their intelligence, inventive capacity, morality, and fitness for the duties of freemen and citizens,—is a doctrine which would find no advocates. No Chancellor of the Exchequer would dare to avow that their sensuality was a prolific source of revenue which he could not afford to check. Why, then, is education to be discouraged by regulations which cut off all aid to children under seven and after eleven years of age? Why are the annual grants to be reduced two-fifths at one blow? Why are the stipends, training, and qualifications of schoolmasters to be lowered? Why is instruction in the school to be mainly concentrated on the three lower elements?

SOURCE: *Four Periods,* pp. 577–578, 599–601, 609–611, 630–635.

Trygve R. Tholfsen is Professor of History at Teachers College, Columbia University. He received his B.A. and Ph.D. from Yale University. He is the author of *Historical Thinking* (New York, 1967) and various articles on Victorian social history, including "The Intellectual Origins of Mid-Victorian Stability," *Political Science Quarterly* (1971).